UNIX™
User's Handbook

Other books in this series
published by Ballantine Books:

UNIX™
User's Handbook

by
WSI Staff

Ballantine Books
New York, NY

This book is available to organizations for special use.
For further information, direct your inquiries to:
Ballantine Books
Special Sales Department
201 East 50th Street
New York, New York 10022

Library of Congress Catalog Card Number: 84-91688
ISBN: 345-32000-X

Manufactured in the United States of America

First Edition: July 1985
10 9 8 7 6 5 4 3 2 1

Contents

Introduction

UNIX User's Handbook is designed to serve as a practical hands-on operating guide to the UNIX operating system. The following topics are discussed in detail:

- History of UNIX
- UNIX design overview
- UNIX system startup and command entry
- File system
- Text editors
- Electronic mail
- File manipulation
- Shell programming
- Communication among UNIX systems
- Text formatting

The reference system used in this text is an IBM PC XT with Santa Cruz Organization's (SCO) version of XENIX. Most of the material presented in this book will apply to other versions of XENIX and UNIX.

Chapter 1 of this book is meant to serve as an introduction to UNIX and XENIX. The history of UNIX is detailed along with an overview of UNIX's structure and a discussion of several different UNIX versions.

In chapter 2, the UNIX system user begins getting hands-on experience. Topics discussed include: login procedure, passwords, and command entry.

UNIX's file and directory system is detailed in chapter 3.

The built-in UNIX text editors ed, ex, and vi are described in detail in chapter 4.

Chapter 5 includes a discussion of UNIX commands used to manipulate files and their data.

UNIX's shell and shell programming are detailed in chapter 6. The mail utility is described in chapter 7. A number of UNIX topics and commands including job control and nroff are detailed in chapter 8.

Our special thanks to Bruce Steinberg of the Santa Cruz Organization, Larry Levine of TC* Services, and Laurie Levine of TC* Services for their assistance in this project. Also, a special acknowledgement goes to Jerry Sadin and August Mohr for their help in editing this book.

1

An Overview

Introduction

In this chapter, we will present an introduction to the UNIX operating system. A short history of UNIX is presented as well as a general overview of the system, and description of several different versions of UNIX.

History Of UNIX

In the late 1960's, Bell Laboratories was partnered with the Massachusetts Institute of Technology (MIT) and General Electric in a project to develop the first interactive, multiuser/ multitasking operating system for implementation on General

Electric's 645 mainframe computer (GE is no longer a computer manufacturer). This operating system was named MULTICS.

An *operating system* is a set of routines that allow the user to communicate more easily with the computer hardware. Typically, the user never communicates directly with the machine. Instead, the user relays instructions to the operating system. The operating system then causes these demands to be carried out by the hardware and reports the results to the user. *Multiuser* refers to a system that allows several individuals to share the use of the computer. *Multitasking* capability enables the computer to appear as if it is working on several tasks at the same time. *Interactive* refers to a system that supports immediate dialogue with the user (as opposed to batch I/O operations involving devices such as card readers, magnetic tapes, etc.).

At the time MULTICS was developed, operating system design was based on the assumption that hardware time was to be conserved at the expense of programming time. MULTICS took a different approach. The system included a large number of programming aids that facilitated programming, but unfortunately slowed hardware operation. MULTICS was too far ahead of its time; it ran too slowly on 1960's vintage hardware.

Bell Labs decided to pull out of the project; MIT and GE continued development. Bereft of the capabilities of MULTICS a young computer scientist, Ken Thompson, working in the computing science research department (Murrary Hill, N.J.) of Bell Labs was forced to move his work to a more affordable minicomputer, the Digital Equipment Corporation (DEC) PDP-7™. Since at the time there was a dearth of software for the PDP-7, Thompson created not only an assembler, but a new file system and primitive operating system to control the system. In a pun on MULTICS, the system was dubbed UNIX by its lone inventor, Thompson. At this point, the UNIX operating system was written in assembly language and limited to use on the PDP-7. This version of UNIX would support only a single user.

Thompson fashioned UNIX to be a software programmer's workshop. Other Bell Labs developers soon became interested in UNIX. One of these, Dennis Ritchie, teamed with Thompson to transfer UNIX to a PDP-11 and set the system up so that it could be used by the Bell Labs patent office as a word processor. This was completed in 1971.

The process of adapting UNIX for a new computer illuminated a very considerable obstacle in software, namely that of *portability*. Portability refers to the ease with which software from one computer system can be moved to others. Assembly languages are very nonportable entities because they are wedded very closely to the architecture of the microprocessor. Since there are many different microprocessors in use, and since new ones are constantly being introduced (with little industry standardization), assembly languages tend to be non-portable and relatively short-lived.

At this time, Thompson was also working on improving programming languages relating to their use in operating systems. For a time, he worked with Basic Combined Programming Language (BCPL), a machine-oriented language designed by Martin Richards at Cambridge in 1967. BCPL is itself a simplification of the verbose Combined Programming Language (CPL). CPL, also a machine-oriented language, was developed in the early 1960's at the University of London and at Cambridge. CPL, in turn, borrows many of its features from the problem-oriented language ALGOL 60. Thompson consolidated BCPL down to its basic features and dubbed the resultant interpreted language B. B, however, had a number of grave shortcomings. Though adequate for the hardware available at the time, B was essentially a very small subset of CPL and as such, had limited applications. Also, B, like its two immediate predecessors, was a machine-oriented language. Machine-oriented languages have historically had poor receptions from applications programmers because generating code in such languages is more difficult.

Dennis Ritchie salvaged the best features of B, changed some of its more restrictive details, added features to it (such as data types and storage classes), and lifted the language above hardware specifics. C was born. C shares some important attributes with UNIX. Since both were created by individuals, they have a coherence and continuity that committee inventions often lack. They are in essence very simple, yet their basic components can be worked in a modular fashion to build units of great authority. Both are flexible and relatively fast.

In 1975, UNIX was rewritten in C making it the first operating system written in a high level language. This version of UNIX, known as version 6, could be transferred to different computers with relative ease. In 1977, UNIX was ported to the Interdata 8/32 and then to the IBM 370.

UNIX version 6 consisted solely of a set of manuals and magnetic tape. Neither support, maintenance nor training were provided, though the package's price was $42,000. Even so UNIX's popularity increased quickly both inside and outside of Bell Labs. UNIX was especially popular at educational institutions due in part to Bell Labs' policy of providing the system to these institutions for a relatively small fee.

UNIX version 7 was released in 1979. It contained a number of new features including an improved C compiler. Version 7 was ported to a number of different computers. A number of enhancements were added at the University of California at Berkeley where UNIX had been ported to VAX minicomputers. This Berkeley version, known as version 4.1, was widely adopted.

UNIX System III was released in 1982. In the early 1980's, a number of UNIX ports were released commercially including XENIX.

In early 1984, Bell Labs released UNIX System V, which included many of the Berkeley version 4.1 enhancements. In the meantime, Berkeley released version 4.2. At this time UNIX shows every indication of becoming a major, if not the standard, small computer operating system of the 1980's.

UNIX Structure

In this section, we'll describe UNIX's basic structure. We'll introduce each of UNIX's major components. These will be discussed in greater detail in later chapters.

HARDWARE ENVIRONMENT

Although UNIX can run on a single user system, it is more typically used on a multiuser system as shown in figure 1.1. A multiuser system of this type generally includes the following components:

- *System hardware* which includes the system's central processor and mass storage units such as disk or tape drives.
- *System console* which is the terminal used to control the system. This terminal is generally also employed as a user terminal.
- *Local user terminals* which are consoles employed by system users to communicate with the system.
- *Remote user terminals* which are consoles connected to the system by modems and phone lines.
- *Communications link* which allows the system to exchange data with other computers.
- *Printers* which are used for outputting hard copy.

Local User Terminals

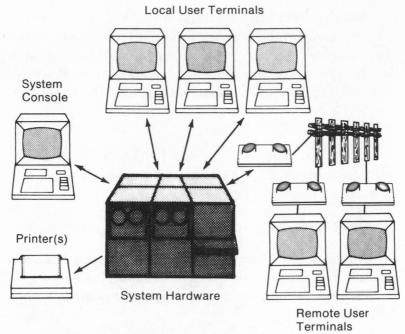

System Console

Printer(s)

System Hardware

Remote User Terminals

Figure 1.1.   Multiuser hardware system

UNIX COMPONENTS

UNIX is comprised of four primary components; the kernel, utilities, the shell, and user processes or programs. These components as well as their interrelationships are depicted in figure 1.2.

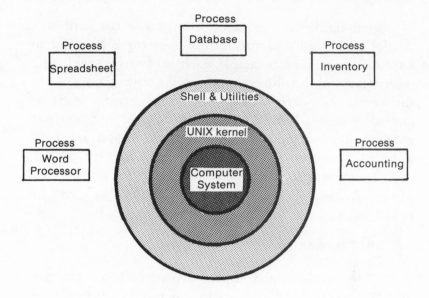

Figure 1.2. UNIX Components

THE KERNEL

The kernel is the heart of the UNIX system. The kernel is invisible to the user. Written in a combination of C and assembler, the kernel is almost identical on different UNIX ports.

The kernel controls the CPU, handles all input and output, runs programs, and alters the memory map. In effect the kernel interfaces directly with the computer hardware leaving the remainder of the UNIX system independent from the hardware. UNIX utilities and processes access the kernel for performance of system functions including:

Memory management	System accounting
Input/output services	Process scheduling
File management	Date and time services
File security	

Since the kernel interfaces directly with the hardware, portions of it must be custom designed for each different hardware system. For example, each hardware system regulates its memory in a different manner. Therefore the portion of the kernel that deals with memory management must be altered for each individual hardware system. Also each system includes different input/output devices. The portion of the kernel that controls these input/output devices, the *drivers*, must be adapted for each individual hardware system. The process of adapting the kernel for individual hardware systems in known as *porting*.

SYSTEM CALLS

UNIX processes and utilities access the kernel through over 60 system calls. A *system call* is an interface between the kernel and the outside utilities and processes that allow these utilities and processes to request that a task be undertaken by the kernel. For example, suppose a process required data that had been input at the terminal. The kernel would be accessed via a system call to retrieve this data.

The system calls are identical on every UNIX system. In effect the system calls create a standard interface between the kernel and outside programs. This standard interface allows processes and utilities to be transported to different UNIX systems without modification.

SHELL

The UNIX shell is the interface between the user and the utilities. It is UNIX's command language and is the portion of UNIX visible to the user at the terminal. The shell can be thought of as a program which communicates with the user and can call other programs. The shell accesses the kernel via the system calls.

A UNIX system often includes more than one shell. For instance many UNIX versions include both the standard Bourne shell as well as the more user-friendly menu oriented C shell.

UTILITIES

UNIX utilities (also known as commands) are a group of over 200 programs written in C that perform specific functions. UNIX utilities include:

- C, FORTRAN77, and Pascal compilers
- Line and screen editors (**ed, sed, vi**)
- Software maintenance tools (**SCCS, make**)
- Electronic mail network (**mail**)
- Text formatting and typesetting (**nroff, troff**)
- File maintenance (**cp**)
- Security (**crypt**)

UNIX system users employ these utilities individually or in combinations to accomplish specific tasks.

A process is in effect an application program. A process is divided into four parts:

- Text (or code) segment which can be shared by several users.
- Data segment which includes program data and variables.
- Run time stack which allows each process to operate independently of the others.
- System segment which contains data used locally by a specific process.

A process can be run in background on a UNIX system by adding an ampersand to the command. This allows other tasks to be carried on during execution of the process.

Different UNIX Versions

A number of different versions of UNIX have been released commercially. These are listed in table 1.1. We will discuss several of these that can be implemented on personal computers here. As a rule a UNIX system includes the following:

- UNIX kernel
- UNIX shell
- Utilities
- C compiler and debugger
- Snobol interpreter
- Available support for other languages such as Basic, Cobol and Pascal.

PC-IX

PC IX is an enhanced version of UNIX System III created by Interactive Systems Corporation of Santa Monica, California. PC IX is designed for use on the PC XT. The total PC IX system includes about 4.5 MB of system software. System features include:

- UNIX shell
- Over 200 utilities including text processing, programming aids, source code system, and games
- Bourne shell
- C compiler & debugger
- Assembler
- Several Berkeley utilities
- Enhanced printer control program (which replaces the System III spooler)
- PC-DOS interface

Table 1.1. UNIX versions

Bell Labs
System V™
System III™
Version 7™
Sixth edition™

Variations of the Bell Labs UNIX	
CPIX™	IBM®
Berkeley version 4.1	Univ of Calif (Berkeley
Berkeley version 4.2	
FOS™	Fortune Systems
Genix®	National Semiconductor
HP-UX®	Hewlitt-Packard
IS/I™	Interactive Systems
OSx™	Pyramid Technology
PC-IX™	Interactive Systems
PERPOS®	Computer Consoles
Sys3™	Plexus
Ultrix™	DEC
Uniplus+™	Unisoft
Unisys®	Codata™
UNITY™	Human Computing Resources
UTS™	Amdahl
VENIX™	VenturCom
XENIX™	Microsoft
Zeus™	Zilog

UNIX Look-alikes	
Coherent™	Mark Williams
Cromix™	Cromemco
Idris™	Whitesmiths Ltd
QNIX™	Quantum Software
UNOS™	Charles River Data

VENIX

Venix is a product of VenturCom (139 Main St. Cambridge, MA 02142). Venix, an enhanced version of the UNIX System III, is available for the IBM PC XT as well as large computers. Venix is widely used for laboratory applications.

UNIPLUS+

Uniplus+ is a product of Unisoft Systems (303 West 42nd St., New York 10036). Uniplus+ is available for 68000 based computers such as the Macintosh XL, NCR Tower, and Sun Workstation. Uniplus+ is an enhanced version of UNIX System III. These enhancements include both Berkeley enhancements as well as some developed by Unisoft.

IDRIS

PC-IX, Venix, and Uniplus+ are all versions of UNIX. A number of operating systems are available that function like UNIX but are not actual versions of the Bell Labs system. Idris, a product of Whitesmiths Ltd. (97 Lowell Rd., Concord, MA 01742), is probably the most widely used UNIX lookalike. Idris is one of the most compact UNIX lookalikes. It can run on an 8080 based system with bank switched memory. Idris is also one of the most portable, running on over 30 different computers.

COHERENT

Coherent is a UNIX lookalike from the Mark Williams Company (1430 W. Wrightwood Ave., Chicago, IL 60614). Coherent is available for the IBM PC as well as systems running the Z8000 and PDP-11. Coherent is a very complete system; it includes nearly as many utilities as UNIX.

XENIX

XENIX is an enhanced version of UNIX System III. These enhancements include a number of Berkeley utilities such as:

- **ex/ed/vi** editors
- **csh** command interpreter
- **style** text analysis program
- **uucp** and **micnet** networking utilities

XENIX was developed by Microsoft Corporation. Microsoft generally does not sell XENIX directly to end-users but instead licenses the system to other firms that customize it for individual hardware products. An exception is the version of XENIX for the PC AT which was ported by Microsoft.

One widely used XENIX port is Santa Cruz Organization's (SCO) XENIX for the IBM PC XT and compatibles. SCO XENIX is marketed as three separate sections:

- XENIX operating system
- XENIX text processing system
- XENIX software development system

The XENIX operating system consists of the UNIX kernal, the C (command) shell, and about 150 utilities including the **ex/ed/vi** editors.

The XENIX text processing system includes most of the features of the UNIX text processing system. The text processing system contains over 20 utility programs including:

- **nroff** for document formatting
- **troff** for outputting formatted documents to a photo-typesetter
- **tbl** for formatting tables
- **eqr** for working with equations
- **style** for analysis of writing style
- **diction** for spotting cumbersome phrasing

The XENIX Software Development System includes a number of programming aids including:

- C compiler
- **lex** and **yacc** program generators
- **make** utility
- **sccs** utility
- 40 additional programming utilities

Unlike PC IX, XENIX is a bonafide multiuser operating system. SCO's implementation of XENIX for the PC XT allows two additional terminals to be added.

As is the case with other UNIX systems, XENIX features multitasking, the ability to run more than one program at a time. XENIX also offers a convenient feature known as virtual consoles. With this feature, the user can alter the keyboard and screen from one program to another by pressing one key. This allows the user to work with several programs at once.

XENIX allows for networking via the **uucp** and **micnet** utilities. These generally transfer information using serial connections and the phone lines or cabling. **uucp** is designed for use with remote systems. **uucp** looks up the remote system's phone numbers, calls them, logs on, relays the information, and logs off — all automatically. **micnet** allows you to connect a small network of local PC's by cable. This is generally used in an office setting. The process is simple; the serial ports on the PC's on the network are connected via cable. **micnet** is also somewhat easier to use than **uucp**, as many of the security problems of a telephone access network are sidestepped.

Due to disk space limitations a number of UNIX features are missing from XENIX. The UNIX games have been omitted as well as the learn utility, an on-line tutorial. Also the on-line manuals were not included.

Even so, XENIX's is probably the most complete version of UNIX available at the time of this writing for personal computers. Also, XENIX is the most widely used version of UNIX on personal computers. An estimated 70% of the installed base of PC's running UNIX in fact run XENIX. Because of this we chose XENIX as the model system for this book.

UNIX Benefits

By now you've probably already recognized some of the benefits of UNIX as compared with other operating systems. In the following sections, we'll identify some of UNIX's many features. These benefits are a major reason why many experts believe that UNIX will emerge as the operating system standard for 16-bit and 32-bit based systems.

BACKGROUND PROCESSING

As we mentioned earlier, UNIX allows background processing whereby the user can execute a program or utility and then continue using the system while that program or utility is running. Background processing allows for more efficient use of the system.

MULTIUSER CAPABILITY

UNIX allows several users to share a computer system while still providing security for each individual user's data and programs. This again allows for more efficient utilization of the computer system.

HARDWARE PORTABILITY

UNIX can be ported to new computer systems with relative ease. Therefore UNIX is available on a wide range of hardware systems. This enables the UNIX user to choose among a number of different hardware systems; he is not locked in with a single vendor.

SOFTWARE PORTABILITY

Since UNIX based applications programs are portable, the same program can be run on a number of different systems. This portability also makes UNIX an attractive environment for software vendors.

PIPES

Pipes are used to connect programs and/or utilities. Piping is a very powerful UNIX feature in that it allows the programmer to combine several simple programs and/or utilities into one complex application. The UNIX programmer using pipes can create complex programs with relative ease.

UNIX UTILITIES

UNIX's over 200 utilities offer a wealth of available information processing power. The utilities can be used for sorting, text processing, networking, file maintenance, and software maintenance. These utilities give UNIX a great deal of flexibility and allow its users to undertake a wide variety of information processing tasks without having to acquire or write programs.

2

Getting Started with UNIX

In this chapter we'll get acquainted with UNIX by actually using the system. We'll learn how to login to the system, execute some simple commands, correct any entry errors and then log off.

Before beginning this discussion however, we need to make some assumptions about the type of terminal and the UNIX shell being used. Also we'll have to obtain some information from the system manager.

Assumptions and Required Information

Your first step is to ask the system manager for your *login name*. This is the name that you will use to identify yourself to the UNIX system. Other system users will require your login name in order to send you messages via UNIX's mail system. When you obtain your login name, you may also be given a password. On multiuser systems, a password is used for security reasons. A system user must know the proper password to access another user's files.

Before logging in, take a few minutes to familiarize yourself with your computer terminal's keyboard. Notice that it is very similar to a typewriter keyboard. Since all keyboards are different, we'll have to make some assumptions about the type of terminal you are using in order to present examples.

One of the most important keys on your terminal's keyboard is the Return key. When the Return key is pressed, the current line is sent to the UNIX system and the cursor moves to the beginning of the next line. Most terminals use the characters RETURN to identify the Return key. Some systems, however, use ENTER or RET. We will indicate pressing the Return key with the following;

[RETURN]

Nearly every terminal has a key that will erase the character just entered. Gererally this key is referred to as the "backspace key." Some terminals actually have a key labelled "Backspace" which performs this function. On most terminals, however, the Control-H key combination is used to delete the character last entered. On a few terminals, the pound sign (#) is used to erase that character. In this book we'll assume that the Control-H key combination is used to erase the character last entered. We'll refer to this key as follows in our examples:

[CTRL-H]

Most keyboards also include a character which can be used to delete the entire line into which characters are being entered. Generally, either the Control-X key combination or the @ key is used to delete an entire line. In this book we'll assume Control-X deletes an entire line, and we'll represent this key combination as:

[CTRL-X]

Another special key that you should be aware of is the interrupt key. This key is used to interrupt the program or utility currently executing. When the interrupt key is pressed, the shell prompt ($ or %) will reappear. On most terminals the Delete key or the Control-C key combination serves as the interrupt key. We'll represent the interrupt key as:

[CTRL-C]

TYPE CONVENTIONS

In order to present information more clearly, we'll use certain type faces in this book to represent program and utility names, keyboard commands, terminal keys, prompts, file-names, screen displays and examples.

When referenced in the text, utility and program names will be presented in the following type style:

who

When a program or utility is used in the context of an entry at the terminal, we will refer to that program or utility as a *command*, and we will indicate it with the following type style:

who

In fact any information entered at the terminal will be displayed in this type style.

Whenever a command is entered at the terminal, the Return key must be pressed to send it to the system. For the sake of clarity we will assume that the reader understands that

[RETURN] is to be pressed at the end of a command and we will not include [RETURN] in our examples.

All screen displays will be illustrated as follows:

```
Welcome to UNIX version 7.1
Login: jetrink
Password:
$
```

Notice that the information entered by the user at the terminal is in a bold type face. The information automatically displayed by UNIX is in a regular type face. The screen outline may be omitted for short displays.

Finally, all filenames will be indicated in the text in bold lowercase letters. They will be indicated as follows when included as part of a command:

memo

UNIX filenames can be indicated in upper case letters, but in this book we will standardize these by using lower case letters exclusively.

C SHELL AND BOURNE SHELL

As discussed in chapter 1, the shell is the interface between the UNIX system and the user. The shell communicates the user's requests to the system and relays the system's responses.

The two most commonly used shells are the Bourne shell and the C shell. The Bourne shell is the standard shell provided with UNIX by Bell Labs. The C shell was developed at the University of California at Berkeley and is included with most Berkeley verions of UNIX.

In this book, we're assuming that the C shell is in use. The easiest way of determining which shell your UNIX system uses is by examining the prompt. If $ is the prompt, the Bourne shell is in use. If % is the prompt, the C shell is being used.

Logging In

Your first step as a UNIX user will be to login to the system. The purpose of logging in is to identify yourself to the UNIX system. Since a number of individuals can use the system, UNIX must be able to identify each system user.

When you sit down at the terminal, your first step generally is to press [RETURN]. A message similar to the following will then be displayed on your terminal screen:

```
Login: _
```

To login just enter your assigned login name and press [RETURN]. You may then be prompted for a password. If your system requires a password (many do not) enter it. The password will not be displayed on the screen for security reasons. If the correct password is entered, the shell prompt will appear as shown on the following page:

```
login: jetrink
password:
Welcome to UNIX for the PC XT!

$
```

The message displayed after a successful login is known as the *message of the day*. This is generally set by the system manager.

If you enter either an incorrect login name or an incorrect password, the following message will be displayed:

login incorrect

ASSIGNING A PASSWORD

After you have successfully logged into the system, you can assign yourself a new password using UNIX's **password** utility. Enter **password** [RETURN]. This command tells the shell to execute the **password** utility. A prompt similar to that depicted in figure 2.1 will appear. You are first prompted to enter your old password. This will prevent another user from changing your password. Once the correct old password has been entered, you will be asked to enter your desired new password. Your password should consist of six to eight characters.

Once you've entered the new password, the **password** utility will request that you reenter it. The purpose of this step is to verify that the new password was correctly entered. Since the password entry is never displayed, if you made a typing error while entering the new password, you would not be able to determine your password. If both new password entries are

```
$ password
Changing password for jetrink
Old password:
Type new password:
Retype new password:

$
```

Figure 2.1. Changing a password

identical, the password will in fact be changed. If they differ, the following message will be displayed:

Mismatch - password unchanged

Notice that the shell prompt is displayed after the error message. You must reexecute the **password** utility in order to make another attempt to change your password.

If you enter a password that is too short, **passwd** responds with:

Please use a longer password

Try using a longer password, from 6 to 8 characters.

Whenever you login, you must enter your password exactly as it was specified in the **passwd** utility. Upper and lower case letters are significant. For example, the following password entries would not match:

beach85
Beach85

If you can't remember your password, contact the system manager for assistance. Although the system manager won't be able to determine your old password, he will be able to assign you a new one.

LOGGING OFF

When you've finished with the UNIX system, you must log off. In order to log off, the shell prompt must be displayed in the current line. Press [Ctrl-D] to log off. The login message should reappear, and the terminal will be ready for the next user.

Correcting Entry Errors

If you notice an entry error, you can correct it as long as [RETURN] has not been pressed. You've two options in correcting entry errors:

1. Delete one character at a time by pressing [CTRL-H] until you reach the character to be corrected.
2. Erase the entire line by pressing [CTRL-X].

Using the Shell

Now that we'll logged into the system, let's begin familiarizing ourselves with UNIX by executing a few simple commands. We'll experiment with **man, who, cal,** and **date**.

man

Many UNIX systems include an on-line manual which can be accessed with the **man** utility. The **man** utility provides on-line information about the utility specified. For example the following command:

man who

would display information about the **who** utility.

With certain **man** displays, only a portion of the entire documentation will be displayed on one screen. A percent value will be displayed on these screens indicating what portion of the entire documentation has been displayed. Press the space bar to access a new data screen. To display one additional line, press [RETURN]. To exit **man** press the interrupt key, [CTRL-C].

who

The **who** utility displays a list of the users currently logged into the UNIX system. The name of the user is displayed along with his terminal device number and the time he logged in.

```
who

joe       tty 02      Jan 04 11:32
bill      tty 03      Jan 04 09:57
steve     tty 05      Jan 04 10:48
```

who can be used with the optional argument **am i** to determine who logged in at the terminal where the command is being executed. If joe executed **who am i**, the following would be displayed on his terminal:

```
who am i
joe          tty 02       04 11:32
```

cal

UNIX's **cal** utility can be used to display a calendar for any year from 0-9999 AD. For example, **cal** could be executed as shown below to display a calendar for 1985:

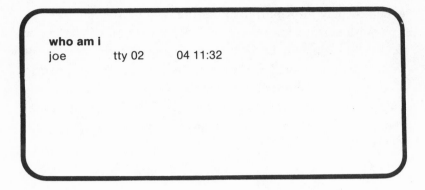

```
$ cal 1985

                          1985
         Jan                   Feb                   Mar
  S  M Tu  W Th  S  S    S  M Tu  W Th  F  S    S  M Tu  W Th  F  S
        1  2  3  4  5                   1  2                   1  2
  6  7  8  9 10 11 12    3  4  5  6  7  8  9    3  4  5  6  7  8  9
 13 14 15 16 17 18 19   10 11 12 13 14 15 16   10 11 12 13 14 15 16
 20 21 22 23 24 25 26   17 18 19 20 21 22 23   17 18 19 20 21 22 23
 27 28 29 30 31         24 25 26 27 28         24 25 26 27 28 29 30
                                              31
```

(We've omitted the remaining months to conserve space.)

cal can also be executed with a number ranging from 01 to 12 preceding the year entry. This number corresponds to one of the 12 months and when included in the command causes the calendar for that month in the indicated year to be displayed.

```
$ cal 04 1985
                    1985
                    Apr
            S   M  Tu  W  Th  F   S
                1   2   3   4   5   6
            7   8   9  10  11  12  13
           14  15  16  17  18  19  20
           21  22  23  24  25  26  27
           28  29  30
```

date

UNIX's **date** command returns the current date and time as shown below:

```
$ date
Wed   Apr   15   12:28:07   EST   1985
```

Special Characters

The following characters have a special meaning in UNIX:

         &   ; | *   ?   \   '   "   '   []   ()   <   >

% and ! are also considered special characters in the C shell.

If you wish to use one of these special characters in its normal context to communicate with the shell, you must quote the character by preceding it with a backslash (\ ) or by enclosing it within a pair of single quotes.

For example suppose you were using,

5*7

as an argument for **expr**, a utility which evaluates an expression.

expr 5*7

would be illegal as the shell would regard * as a special character rather than as the symbol for the multiplication operation. The command would have to be specified as:

expr 5 *7

3

The UNIX File System

In this chapter we'll discuss the organization of UNIX's file system. We'll discuss the overall structure of the UNIX file system, the directory system, and a number of file handling commands.

Files & Filenames

The fundamental unit which is used to store information in UNIX is the *file*.

A file is a group of related information. For example, a file might consists of a list of all the names, addresses, and phone numbers of your customers. A file might also contain the text of a standard form letter you send to sales prospects. A file could also contain a set of programming instructions to edit and print text data.

The advantage of grouping information in a file is that it can be easily retrieved by UNIX and can be stored on disk when it is not being used.

Every file is assigned a *filename*. UNIX filenames can consist of from 1 to 14 characters. Any character* can be used in a filename although by convention UNIX filenames generally include the following characters:

> Uppercase letters (A-Z)
> Lowercase letters (a-z)
> Numbers (0-9)
> Period (.)
> Comma (,)
> Underline character (_)

UNIX distinguishes between upper and lower case letters in filenames. Therefore,

> Memo.to.sam
> memo.to.sam
> Memo.to.Sam

would each be perceived by UNIX as different filenames.

Again, it is advisable to avoid using characters that have a special meaning in UNIX as part of a filename (see page 39).

Also don't insert a blank space within a filename. When UNIX encounters a blank space in a filename or a command, it interprets that as the end of the filename or command. Use a period or the underline character rather than a blank space to separate portions of a filename. For example, **memo.to.sam** should be specified rather than **memo to sam** to denote a single file.

---

* The exception to this rule is that no file can be named /. As we'll see later / is used to refer to the root directory.

When a filename is separated by a period in this manner, the portion of the filename appearing after the period is known as the *filename extension*. Filename extensions are useful in creating filenames that are easy to understand.

UNIX Directory System

A UNIX system can contain hundreds or even thousands of files. Obviously a structure must be in place to efficiently keep track of these numerous files. UNIX organizes individual files by grouping them in directories. A directory can be thought of as a file drawer in a filing cabinet. Just as the file drawer contains a number of individual file folders, a UNIX directory contains a number of individual files.

UNIX directories and files are organized in a hierarchical structure, a system where items are linked together in a top-down fashion. An organization chart is a good example of a hierarchical structure. In the remainder of this section, we'll describe UNIX file and directory organization by depicting it as an organization chart (see figure 3.1).

The directory system depicted in figure 3.1 has 5 separate levels. It is not uncommon for a UNIX directory system to have 9 or 10 separate levels. A discussion of these 5 levels will, however, be sufficient to portray the structure of the directory system.

At the top of the directory hierarchy lies the *root* directory. The root directory serves as a reference point for all the other directories. It is represented by the slash symbol (/).

The various components of the UNIX system are stored in directories in level 2 of the directory system directly below the root directory. These directories include:

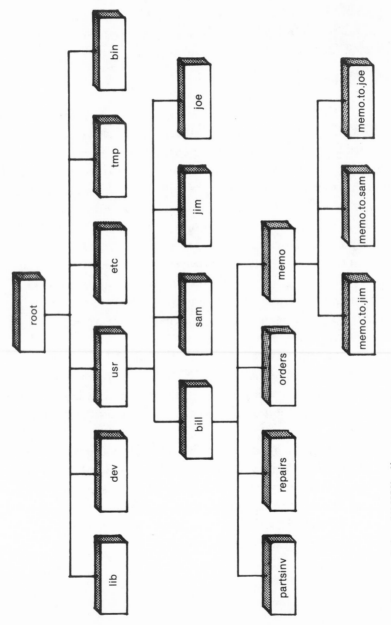

Figure 3.1. UNIX's directory system

bin   which is used to store the UNIX utilities.

lib   which contains libraries used by UNIX.

tmp   which contains temporary files.

etc   which contains administrative programs such as **passwd**.

dev   which contains files which represent devices.

usr   which contains user files.

Each of these component directories can in turn hold additional directories and eventually files. These additional directories are known as *subdirectories*. As you can see from figure 3.1, a subdirectory can have a subdirectory of its own. For example, **memo.to.sam** is a file which is contained in **memo**, which is a subdirectory of bill's directory, which is a subdirectory of **usr** which is a component directory of **root**.

In this chapter we're going to concentrate on the **usr** component directory, as that portion of the UNIX file system is the most widely used. In the UNIX file system, every user is assigned a *home* directory, which contains the file created by that user.

When you login to the UNIX system, your home directory will be your *working* or *current* directory. The working directory can be defined as the directory you are currently working from. The **cd** (change directory) utility can be used to change the working directory.

If there is ever any confusion as to which directory is the current working directory, the **pwd** utility can be used to display the present working directory on the screen.

Suppose Bill just logged into the system. If Bill executed **pwd** the screen would resemble the following:

```
login: bill
password:
Welcome to UNIX
$pwd
/usr/bill
$
```

The last directory name displayed by **pwd** is the working directory. **/usr/bill** is known as a pathname.

You've probably already wondering, "How does UNIX know where to find a file?" We'll show how pathnames are used to reference files in the next section.

FULL PATH NAMES

To specify a particular file or directory in the UNIX file system, a full path name is used. A full path name is an expression that uniquely specifies a file or directory. A full path name always starts from the root directory. Each directory that appears in the directory system between the root directory and the desired file directory is then listed, successively. After the root directory, all subsequent names appearing in the full path name are separated by a slash. The slash used as a separator should not be confused with the name of the root directory, which is also / . For example, the full path name for **memo.to.- sam** depicted in figure 3.1 is:

/usr/bill/memo/memo.to.sam

Note that this convention for specifying files allows files that appear in different directories to share the same name. Study figure 9.1 carefully; note that the name **bin** is used twice.

However, the two occurrences of **bin** are distinguishable from each other because they have different full path names. One has the full path name:

/bin

The other's full path name is:

/usr/bin

This distinguishability is convenient. Individual users need not worry if another person has already used a name when creating a file. As long as a user has not previously used the name for one of his own files, the file will have a unique name specified by the full path name.

Notice that the directories and filenames in our examples can't be distinguished. UNIX does not differentiate filenames and directory names. Many users arbitrarily begin the first character of the directory names with a capital letter so they can distinguish these from filenames.

RELATIVE PATH NAMES AND SEARCH PATHS

Specifying a full path name for each file or directory that is needed could become a tedious task. UNIX therefore allows the use of relative path names. These specify a file or directory relative to the current directory.

Search paths make using relative path names practical; they are used to simplify name specifications. A search path is a list of partial full path names.

Each of the partial path names begin at the root directory. When a relative path name of a file or directory is specified, the first partial path name in the list is added to the specified name. This action creates a full path name. This full path name is searched for. If the specified file directory is found, the search ends, successfully. If the file or directory is not found, the next partial path name in the search path is used. If all of the partial path names in the search path are exhausted and the file or directory has still not been found, the search terminates unsuccessfully. An error message stating this fact will appear on the screen.

The search path for each individual user is specified in his **.profile** file. A search path typically includes the following partial path names:

. This indicates the current working directory as the partial pathname.

/bin This allows the user to access utilities.

/usr/bin This allows the user to access additional utilities.

DISPLAYING DIRECTORY INFORMATION

UNIX includes three commands that will cause information about a directory to be displayed, **l, ls,** and **lc.** All three commands are similar. We will discuss only the **ls** command.

Type **ls** and press the Return key. This action will cause the names of all the regular files and directories contained in the current directory to be displayed. One name will be displayed on each line. If the current directory is empty, the message "total 0" will be displayed.

Information about a directory other than the current directory can be obtained by including that directory's name as an argument to the **ls** command. For example, to display the contents of the root directory on the screen, type **ls /** and press the Return key. A display similar to the following will appear:

```
bin
dev
etc
lib
lost+found
mnt
once
tmp
usr
xenix
```

Note that the names are alphabetically sorted.

More information about each file or directory can be obtained. The -l option causes a long version of the ls output to be generated. This long version will have the format illustrated in figure 3.2. The access permission for each file is broken into three categories. Each category can be allowed or denied read, write, and execute permission. A dash in the permission field indicates that the permission is denied. An "r" indicates read permission is allowed. A "w" indicates write permission is allowed. And, an "x" indicates execute permission is allowed.

In the example in figure 3.2, the file is a directory. The file's owner, root, has read, write and execute permission to the file. Execute permission is equivalent to search permission for a directory. The file's group, also root, has only read and execute permission to the file. All other users also have only execute permission to the file.

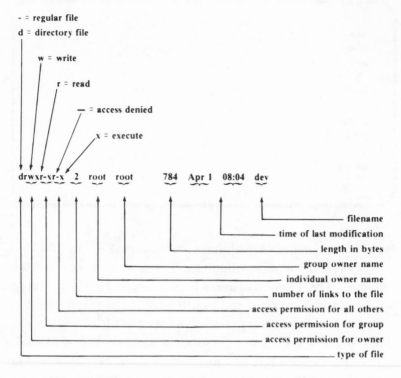

Figure 3.2. Format of the output from an **ls -l** command.

To display the long version of the **ls** command, type **ls -l /** and press the Return key. The screen display will resemble the following:

```
total 125
drwxr-xr-x    2 bin     bin        1824 Apr  1 08:05 bin
drwxr-xr-x    2 root    root        768 Apr  1 08:04 dev
drwxr-xr-x    3 bin     bin         784 Apr  1 13:31 etc
drwxr-xr-x    2 bin     bin          48 Apr  1 07:58 lib
drwxr-xr-x    2 root    root       1328 Apr  1 08:07 lost+found
drwxrwxrwx    2 root    root         32 Apr  1 08:04 mnt
drwxrwxrwx    2 root    root         48 Apr  1 08:07 once
drwxrwxrwx    2 root    root         96 Apr  2 01:37 tmp
drwxr-xr-x   15 bin     bin         240 Apr  1 13:31 usr
-rw-r--r--    1 bin     bin      113856 Apr  1 00:00 xenix
```

In addition to the -l option, several other options are available. These options may be used to sort the display in a different manner (by time of last modification, reverse order, etc.), to give slightly different information (inode number, size in blocks) or to include hidden files in the display. Hidden files are those that start with a period. The **.profile** file is an example of a hidden file.

CHANGING DIRECTORIES

Movement within the UNIX file system can be accomplished by changing the current working directory. Changing directories is most useful when extensive work is to be done in a subdirectory of the home directory. Changing the directory to a lower level will save specifying the higher level directories in the path name each time a file is accessed.

For example, in figure 3.1 the directory **bill** includes the subdirectory **memo.** If Bill needed to perform extensive work on the files **memo.to.jim** and **memo.to.sam**, he could change the current directory to **memo.** Now, only the filename need be specified instead of the partial path **memo/***filename.*

The **cd** command causes the current working directory to be changed. The command has the form:

cd *directory name*

where *directory name* is the name of the directory to be changed to. The directory name can be either a full path name or a partial path name that can be found in the search path.

To go to a higher directory, the full path name must be given. To get to the command directory, /**bin,** type **cd** /**bin** and press the Return key. The **cd** command does not generate a message on the screen. To list the contents of the new working directory, use the **ls** command. To return to the home directory, type **cd** and press the Return key. The **cd** command with no argument specified will always return the working directory to the user's home directory, no matter where in the file system the current working directory is located. To move to a subdirectory such as **memo** in figure 3.1, if the current directory is **/usr/jim** type **cd memo** and press the Return key.

An important point to remember is that changing the current working directory causes the search path to be changed. Each directory has a different . entry. This dot entry provides the search path not included in the **/bin** and **/usr/bin** portion.

CREATING A SUBDIRECTORY

An individual user can arrange his own directory by creating subdirectories. These subdirectories can be used to store related files. In this manner, data relating to a particular job can be isolated in a single subdirectory. For example, a person in charge of keeping records for several different stores could create subdirectories named after each store. Each subdirectory would contain the data files for that store, such as volume, personnel, and inventory files.

The **mkdir** (make directory) command is used to create a directory. This command has the following form:

mkdir *directory name*

where *directory name* represents the name, unique within the user's current directory, of the new directory. Be aware that directory names, like file names are limited to 14 characters. For example, to create a subdirectory for a store located in Lakewood, Bill could type:

mkdir lkwd

and press the Return key. The path for the new directory would be:

/usr/bill/lkwd

The **mkdir** utility displays no messages if the directory is created.

If the user does not have write access to the current working directory and attempts to create a directory, the following error message will be displayed on the screen:

mkdir: cannot access.

The directory will not be created. Generally, individual users should create subdirectories only in their home directory.

REMOVING A SUBDIRECTORY

Subdirectories that are no longer needed should be removed from the system. This removal provides the system with more free storage space.

The **rmdir** (remove directory) utility can be used to remove an empty directory. An empty directory contains no files except the hidden files. The command has the following form:

rmdir *directory name*

where *directory name* represents the name of the directory to be removed. The **rmdir** command is considered the safe way to delete a directory because each individual file must be removed before the directory can be erased. A more risky command is the recursive remove:

rm -r *directory name*

This command causes all the files and subdirectories in the specified directory to be deleted. The directory itself will then be removed. Do not invoke this command unless you are absolutely certain the current directory is where you want this action to take place. Substantial loss of data can occur if this command is misused.

Files

Unlike directories, UNIX files can contain only data. This data can be executable programs, text, numbers or any other valid data type. In a working XENIX system, the files will substantially outnumber the directories.

CREATING A FILE

Files can be created in many different ways. The most common method of creating a file is through the use of a text editor. Another common method of creating a new file is through a program that opens a file, writes data to that file, and eventually closes that file. A third method, which we'll discuss in the next section involves the output redirection operator (>). When a file is created, it will be entered into the current working directory. If the user does not have permission to write in the current working directory, an error message will appear on the screen and the file will not be created. Generally, individual users should create files only in their home directory.

USING THE OUTPUT REDIRECTION OPERATOR TO CREATE A FILE

In the next chapter we'll learn how to create files using the UNIX editors. If you want to experiment with file creation; you can easily do so by using the output redirection operator (>). The > operation tells the shell that output is to be redirected from the terminal to a file. The > operator is used with the following configuration:

command [arguments] > filename

command can be a UNIX utility or application program. *argument* refers to optional command argumetns. *filename* refers to the file to which the data is being redirected. You should exercise caution when using the output redirection operator. If the *filename* specified duplicates that of an existing file, the existing file will be erased.

Suppose we wanted to create a text file named **data1.txt**. We could use the **cat** utility with the output redirection operator as shown below to create such a file and write data to it.

```
$ cat > data1.txt
This is the first line
We now have two lines
Press Control-D to end.
[CTRL-D]
$
```

data1.txt will contain the three lines entered via the keyboard. If you want to examine the file enter:

```
$cat data1.txt
This is the first line
We now have two lines.
Press Control-D to end.
$
```

Notice that when the **cat** command is specified with a filename but without the output redirection operator, that file will be displayed on the terminal.

DISPLAYING FILE CONTENTS

As shown in the last section, **cat** can be used to display a short file on the screen. **cat** is not as useful for displaying longer files, as if the entire file will not fit on the screen, its contents will scroll by.

To view long files, the **more** utility provides a more satisfactory display. The **more** utility displays the first screen of data and stops. The user controls scrolling through the file. The command to use the **more** utility has the following form:

more *filename*

where *filename* is the name of the file to be displayed. For example, to view the long file, **/etc/termcap,** type:

more /etc/termcap

and press the Return key. The beginning of the **/etc/termcap** file will be displayed on the screen. The last line will display the percentage of the file that has been viewed so far. Typing a carriage return will cause the file to scroll up one line. Pressing the space bar will display another full screen of text.

COPYING FILES

At times, a copy of an existing file is needed. The **cp** utility is used to accomplish the job of making a copy of a file. The **cp** command has the form:

cp   *sending file   receiving file*

where *sending file* represents the name of the file to be copied, and *receiving file* represents the name of the file to receive the copy. The receiving file will be created if it does not exist. The receiving file will be overwritten if it does exist.

For example, if Bill and Sam are members of the same group, Sam can obtain a copy of Bill's file **memo.to.sam** by typing:

cp /usr/bill/memo/memo.to.sam   mycopy

and pressing the Return key. This command will cause a file named **mycopy** to be added to Sam's directory. Note that Sam must have read access permission to Bill's files in order for the copy to be successfully made.

LINKING FILES

In the last example, Sam obtained a copy of Bill's file **memo.to.sam**. If Bill updated his **memo.to.sam** file, Sam's copy of the file, **mycopy**, would become outdated. To resolve this problem, the two files can be linked.

Only one copy of a linked file is stored in the UNIX system. This file will appear under a different name in the directory of each user who owns a link to the file. Anyone who owns a link to the file can change the file providing they have write permission for that file. The updated version of the file immediately becomes available to all the other users who own links to the file.

For the link to work properly, the access permission of the file must be changed so that the users with links appearing in their directory can modify the file. The **chmod** utility* can be used to accomplish the task of modifying the access permission. To allow his other group members to link to the file **memo.to.sam**, Bill should type:

chmod g+w memo.to.sam

---

* We'll discuss **chmod** in more detail later in this chapter.

and press the Return key. If this step is not taken, only Bill will be able to change the linked file.

The **ln** utility is used to establish a link. This command has the following form:

ln *original new*

where *original* represents the name of the file to be linked and *new* represents the name of the new link to that file. For example, Sam would type:

ln /usr/bill/memo/memo.to.sam mycopyb

and press the Return key to obtain a link to Bill's **memo.to.sam** file in his home directory. The link would appear as **mycopyb** in Sam's home directory.

Now, whenever either Sam or Bill changes the linked file, both users will have access to the new, updated version.

MOVING (OR RENAMING) A FILE

UNIX's **mv** utility allows the user to move or rename a file. **mv** can be used as follows to rename a file or directory.

mv *oldfilename newfilename*

Here, **mv** is used to simply rename a file. Be careful when using **mv** to rename file. If your *newfilename* duplicates that of an existing file, that file will be erased.

mv can also be used as follows to move one or more files to another directory.

mv *filea fileb... directory*

In order for **mv** to be used to move files, the *directory* specified must exist, and the user must have write access to that directory.

Suppose you executed the following command:

mv chapter book

UNIX would first determine whether or not a directory existed with the name **book**. If such a directory did exist, **chapter** would be placed in that directory. If it did not exist, **chapter** would be renamed as **book**.

SEARCHING A FILE

grep is one of UNIX's most useful utilities. **grep** searches one or more files for a specified character string. **grep** will print out those lines that contain the specified character string. **grep** is used as follows:

grep *searchstring filea fileb...*

searchstring indicates the characters **grep** is to search for. If *searchstring* includes a blank character, it must be enclosed in single quotes so that UNIX will not interpret the portion of the *searchstring* occurring after the blank space as a filename. *filea* and *fileb* indicate the files to be searched.

Suppose you had a data file that contained the names and address of the alumni of your school. You could print out the line in the file containing Jim Reger's name by using **grep** as follows;

$**grep** 'Jim Reger' **alumni.dat**

Wildcard characters (discussed in a later section) can be used in the *searchstring*.

Removing a File

When a file is no longer needed, it should be removed. Removing unneeded files frees storage space for other users.

The **rm** command is used to remove files. The user trying to remove a file must have write access for the directory that contains that file. If he does not, an error message will be generated, and the file will not be deleted. Generally, an individual user should remove only files in his home directory. The **rm** command has the following form:

rm *filename*

where *filename* represents the name of the file to be removed. More than one filename can be specified. Each filename should be separated by a blank. For example, the following command:

rm sales inventory

would cause the files **sales** and **inventory** to be removed from the current working directory.

CHARACTER AND PATTERN MATCHING CHARACTERS

UNIX includes two character matching characters (? and *) as well as the pattern matching sequence [ ]. The advantage of using these characters in your commands is that you can specify a number of filenames or data items with just one entry.

? matches any single character. Suppose your current directory contained the following files:

memo.to.joe	**memo.to.bill**
memo.to.sally	**memo.to.hal**
memo1	**memo3**
memo2	**memo.to.rich**

You could list **memo1, memo2,** and **memo3** to the line printer by using the ? character as follows:

$lpr memo?[1]

The * matches any zero or more characters in a filename. For example,

$lpr memo*

would send all of the filenames in our current directory to the printer. The following command

$lpr *

would have an identical effect. * matches every filename except for those that begin with a period (such as **.profile**). The following command:

$lpr memo.*

would send:

memo.to.joe   **memo.to.bill**
memo.to.sally   **memo.to.hal**

to the printer.

One or more characters enclosed in brackets can be used to denote a number of characters that can be used to match a single character in the filename. For example if the current directory included,

texta.dat   **text1.dat**   **text7.dat**
textb.dat   **textz.dat**   **textd.dat**
textg.dat   **text3.dat**

---

[1]**lpr** is a UNIX utility that sends the specified file to the line printer.

the following command,

$lpr text[abc].dat

would send the following files to the printer:

texta.dat
textb.dat

Characters can also be specified as a range using [ ]'s. For example,

$lpr text[a-g].dat

would send the following files to the printer:

texta.dat	**textg.dat**
textb.dat	**textd.dat**

A numeric range can also be specified. The following command,

$lpr text [1-9].dat

would send:

text1.dat	**text3.dat**
text7.dat	

to the printer.

File Access

Each file has three levels of user access: the *owner*, the *group* to which the owner belongs, and the *other* users. Each file can be accessed in three different ways. The file can be *read* from, *written*, to or *executed*. UNIX, therefore, allows three types of access for each of the three different user types making nine file access permissions overall. The different access permissions are depicted in figure 3.3.

The file owner determines who has what access to his files. As mentioned earlier, the **ls** command an be used with the l option to display a file's access permissions.

UNIX's file access feature allows an individual to control who has access to his files. Keep in mind, however, that the system manager can login as the *super user* and can access all files regardless of the stated access.

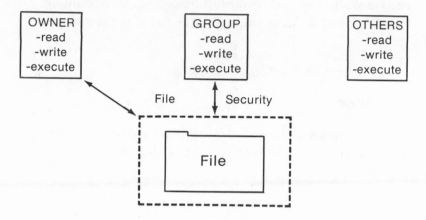

Figure 3.3. File access permissions

UNIX includes several utilities that can be used to set or affect the access permissions. These include:

chown
chgrp
chmod
newgrp
su

We will discuss these utilities individually in the following sections.

chown & chgrp

chown (change owner) is used to change the individual ownership of a file while **chgrp** (change group) is used to change the group ownership of a file. These commands are used with the following configurations:

> **chown** *individualname filename*
> **chgrp** *groupname filename*

Suppose we wanted to change the individual ownership of **receivables** to tom and the group ownership to accounting. We could do so by executing the following commands:

> **chown** tom **receivables**
> **chgrp** accounting **receivables**

chmod

The **chmod** (change mode) utility is used to change a file's access permissions. **chmod** is used with the following configuration.

> **chmod** {*ugoa*} {+-} {*rwx*}

u specifies the user or owner's login name, *g* specifies a group, and *o* indicates all others. *a* indicates the user, group and all others; it is the default. + adds permission; - deletes permission. *r* indicates read, *w* indicates write, and *x* indicates execute.

For example the following command:

> **chmod** go-w **memo.to.bill**

would disallow write access for the group and all others to the file named **memo.to.bill**.

newgrp

The **newgrp** (new group) utility can be executed to change a user's active group. If Bill entered the following command:

$newgrp committee1

his active group would be changed to committee1. **newgrp** verifies that the user is a member of the specified group before allowing that group as his active group.

su

UNIX's **su** (super user) utility allows a user to assume another user's identity without logging off and then logging back on. This allows one user to access another's files temporarily.

If Bill was logged into the system, the following command,

$su joe

would allow Bill to temporarily assume Joe's identity. Bill would then be able to access Joe's files. Bill could reassume his own identity by pressing [CTRL-D]

If the specified user name requires a password, **su** will request that password. If a user name is not specified with **su**, the user executing the command will assume super-user status.

ADVANCED TOPICS

The material that we discuss in this section can be skipped by the novice user. Knowledgeable users will find the information in this section useful for completing specific tasks. Topics in this section include the use of the creation mask, how to create and mount another file system, how to format diskettes, and how to store specific files on a diskette.

Creation Mask

The UNIX system uses the file creation mask to set the access permissions for a file when it is created. The default value for the mask is set in the **.profile** file. The default value of the file creation mask assigns the following access permissions:

files   **rw-r--r--**

directories   **rwx-xr-x**

For files, these permissions represent read and write for the file owner and read only for both the group and all others. For directories, these permissions represent read, write and search for the directory owner and read and search for the group and for all others.

The file creation mask can be modified so that a different set of access permissions will be assigned. The user accessible part of the creation mask contains three octal digits. An octal digit can have a value from 0 to 7. One of the three digits controls access permission for the owner, another for the group, and the last for all others. Table 3.1 lists the access permissions related to each octal digit. The default creation mask that is specified in the user's **.profile** file is:

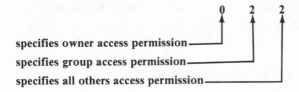

This mask specifies read and write permission for the owner and read permission for the group and others.

The **umask** utility allows the individual user to specify a new creation mask. The current value of the creation mask can be checked by typing:

umask

and pressing the Return key. This command will cause four digits to be displayed on the screen. The rightmost three digits specify the file creation mask as we discussed earlier. The command to change the file creation mask has the following form:

umask *ugo*

where *u* represents the access permission for the owner, *g* represents the access permission for the group and *o* represents the access permission for all others.

For example, if the file creation mask has not been changed, typing **umask** and pressing the Return key will cause the screen to display:

0022

This is the default creation mask that we discussed earlier. If it is desirable to disallow users outside of the group (others) from access to the file, type:

umask 027

and press the Return key. This new setting of the creation mask will disallow others from accessing any files and directories created while it is in force.

An important point to remember when using the **umask** command is that the command affects the access permissions assigned to files as they are created. The **umask** command does not change the access permission of files already in existence. The **chmod** utility will change the access permission of existing files. Examples showing how to use the **chmod** utility were presented earlier in this chapter.

Table 3.1. Access permissions related to the octal digits in the creation mask.

Octal Digit		Access Permission	Description
0	file	rw-	read and write
	directory	rwx	read, write, and execute
1	file	rw-	read and write
	directory	rw-	read and write
2	file	r--	read
	directory	r-x	read and execute
3	file	r--	read
	directory	r--	read
4	file	-w-	write
	directory	-wx	write and execute
5	file	-w-	write
	directory	-w-	write
6	file	---	none
	directory	--x	execute
7	file	---	none
	directory	---	none

Storing Information on Diskettes

Information that is used infrequently should be stored on floppy disks. This infrequently used data can then be removed from the UNIX file system. This procedure helps free more storage space for use within the file system.

Also, a special diskette containing certain files could be made up to satisfy a specific need. For example, a diskette could be prepared to contain all the files pertaining to a completed project. This diskette could be stored with the project records. The files could then be removed from the system.

FORMATTING DISKETTES

Before a diskette may be used to store files in the UNIX system, the diskette must be initialized. This initialization procedure is known as formatting the diskette. Formatting a diskette destroys any data that was previously stored on the diskette.

The **format** command is used to format a diskette. To format a diskette, type:

format

and press the Return key. The screen will display:

Insert floppy in drive
Hit return when ready.

The diskette should now be inserted into the floppy drive. After closing the drive door, press the Return key. The screen will display:

formatting /dev/format 0 ...

When the formatting process is complete, the screen will display:

formatting /dev/format 0 ... done

and the shell prompt will appear on the screen.

The diskette is now ready to be used to store information.

COPYING SPECIFIC FILES TO A DISKETTE
CREATING A UNIX FILE SYSTEM ON A DISKETTE

A UNIX file system can be created on a floppy diskette. This is often a useful way to store working files. The floppy file system can be made accessible to the root file system using the **mount** command.

The file system is necessary to organize the files on the diskette. The **mkfs** utility is used to create the file system on the diskette. This command has the following form:

/etc/mkfs   *device file   size   gap   block*

where *device file* represents the special device file name. *size* represents the total number of data blocks available to the new file system, *gap* represents the gap number for the disk. *block* represents the block number for the disk. On the IBM PC XT, the name of the floppy drive is **/dev/fd0**. For the standard floppy drive in an IBM PC XT, the command to create a file system on a diskette is:

/etc/mkfs /dev/fd0 320 2 8

Once the file system has been created, it must be mounted into the UNIX root file system. This action must be taken so that the operating system can assign path names from the **root** directory to the new file system. Without path names, the new file system is inaccessible.

The **mount** utility is used to mount a file system into the UNIX root file system. The **mount** utility along with the corresponding **umount** utility (used for unmounting file systems), can be invoked by individual users. However, if you find the **mount** and **umount** utilities restricted to use by the superuser, talk to the system manager to find out if the access permissions can be changed.

If the access permissions have been changed to allow individual users to execute the **mount** and **umount** utilities, mount the new file system as outlined below. Otherwise, have the system manager mount it.

A new file system must be mounted into an empty directory. An empty directory is a directory that contains only the hidden files . and ... The /**mnt** directory is an empty directory that has been created for the express purpose of temporarily mounting file systems. Also, since the diskette may have to be used by a variety of people, all files created on the diskette should allow access to every system user. To allow access to every system user, issue the **umask** utility to change the file creation mask. Specify a creation mask of **000**.

The command to mount a file system has the form:

/etc/mount *device name* *directory name*

where *device name* represents the name of the special device file for the device that contains the new file system. *directory name* represents the full path name of the empty directory through which the new file system is to be accessed. For example, the following command:

/etc/mount **/dev/fd0** **/mnt**

would cause the file system on the diskette loaded into the floppy disk drive 0 to be mounted on the /**mnt**.

The new file system can now be used exactly like any other portion of the UNIX file system. The directory in which the file system is mounted provides the entry point to the new file system. Files can be created on the diskette using text editors, moved to or from the diskette using the **mv** utility, and copied to or from the diskette using the **cp** or **copy** utilities.

When all the tasks using the new file system have been completed, the new file system should be unmounted. The **umount** utility is used to unmount file systems. The command to unmount a file system has the following form:

/etc/umount *device name*

where *device name* represents the name of the special device file for the device that contains the mounted file system. For example, the following command:

/etc/umount   /dev/fd0

would cause the file system contained on the diskette loaded into floppy drive 0 to be unmounted.

After the file system has been unmounted, the file creation mask should be changed back to its original configuration.

NOTE FOR THE SYSTEM MANAGER

The following two choices regarding the use of the **mount** and **umount** utilities are available:

1. Each time a file system must be mounted or unmounted, login as the super-user and perform the steps necessary to mount or unmount the file system. These steps are detailed in the text.

2. Change the access permission on the **/etc/mount** and **/etc/umount** files so that individual users can execute these files. To accomplish these changes, login as the super-user and issue the following commands:

   chmod o+x /etc/mount

   chmod o+x /etc/umount

4

ed, ex & vi Text Editors

A text editor is a program that allows the user to create or change a file. The process of changing a file is called editing. UNIX users can choose among several text editors. UNIX systems generally include three text editors: **ex, ed,** and **vi.** .

ex and **ed** are both line editors. Our examples in this chapter were generated using the **ed** line editor. These commands also apply to **ex**, however. The major difference between **ex** and **ed** is that **ex** includes a few additional features.

The **vi** utility is a full screen editor also included in most UNIX versions. A full screen editor allows an entire screen, typically 20 to 25 lines, to be viewed at once. Any of the displayed data can be edited. Once proficiency in the use of **vi** is gained, the payoff is quicker completion of tasks, in comparison to **ed**.

ed — A LINE EDITOR

Invoking ed

The line editor **ed,** can be entered in either of two manners. The first is to simply type **ed** and press the Return key. This command will cause the editor to be invoked. The screen will display an asterisk (*). The asterisk is the line editor prompt. This prompt signifies that the **ed** utility is waiting for some command from the user. If the prompt does not appear, type **P** and press the Return key. The **P** command turns on and off the prompt. All the line editor commands described in the following sections must be entered immediately following the asterisk prompt. (If the prompt is turned off, the commands will still work, but we will assume that the prompt is on to avoid confusion.)

The line editor can also be invoked with a specification that a certain file be edited. The command to enter the **ed** utility in this manner has the following form:

ed *filename*

where *filename* is the name of the file to be edited. When **ed** is invoked in this fashion, a number will be displayed on the line before the asterisk prompt. This number represents the number of characters in the file that was specified for editing. If the specified file does not exist, a zero will appear for the number of characters in the file.

One point that is important to note is that the editor does not work directly on the contents of a file. Instead, the editor automatically makes a temporary copy of the file being edited in a buffer. A buffer is a temporary storage area. The file being edited is not actually altered until a command to write the changes is issued. If a new file is being created, the file does not exist except in this buffer until a write command is given.

For example, the following command:

ed results

would cause the line editor to be invoked and a copy of the file **results** to be loaded into the editing buffer. Changes made during the editing session would not be saved in the file **results** until a **write** command is issued.

Exiting ed

The quit command is used to exit from the **ed** utility. The quit command is issued when an asterisk prompt is displayed, by typing **q** and pressing the Return key. If changes have been made on the current file and not saved, the screen will display the following message:

?
warning: expecting w'

Issuing another quit command will cause an exit from the **ed** utility without the changes in the file being saved.

The warning message is a safety feature. It helps the user to remember to save all the editing changes made during the editing session. The feature helps to avoid accidental loss of completed work. Note that if a new file is currently being edited and the double quit is used to exit the line editor without saving the file, the new file will not appear in the file system. The file was never actually created. It existed only as a temporary file in the editor's buffer area. If only a question mark is displayed, type **H** and press the return key. The **H** command turns on and off the explanation of error messages. If error messages are turned off, the **h** command can be used to display the explanatory message.

Saving Edited Files

The write command is used to save the edited copy of the file. When a write command is issued, the file stored in the editor's buffer is used to overwrite the file stored (after the asterisk prompt) in the file system. To execute a write command, type **w** and press the Return key. This causes the contents of the buffer to overwrite the currently specified file. The currently specified file is the name (if any) given when the line editor was invoked.

If no file is currently specified, issuing a write command will cause the following error message to be displayed on the screen.

?

illegal or missing filename

FINDING THE CURRENTLY SPECIFIED FILE

The name of the currently specified file can be displayed on the screen using the file command. Type **f** and press the Return key. The screen will display the name of the currently specified file. If there is no currently specified file, no filename will be displayed.

CHANGING THE CURRENTLY SPECIFIED FILE

The currently specified file can be changed to a different file using the file command. This usage of the file command has the following form:

f *filename*

where *filename* represents the name of the file that should be made the currently specified file.

For example, the following commands:

f newresults

w

would cause the currently specified file to be changed to **newresults**. The contents of the editing buffer would then be used to create or overwrite the file **newresults**, depending on whether the file existed before the write command was executed.

Moving Within the File

The **ed** utility keeps track of which line in the buffer is the current line. Generally, a line is the text or data that is displayed on one line of the screen. The current line is the line that will be affected by any editing commands that are issued. The current line is represented by a period (.). The current line is often called "line dot" or simply "dot". Initially, the current line is set to the first line in the file. Pressing the Return key will display the next line and advance the current line number. The first line is line number one. Subsequent lines are numbered sequentially. The current line number can be displayed by typing .= and pressing the Return key.

MOVING TO A SPECIFIC LINE NUMBER

The current line can be changed to a different line number by typing a line number and pressing the Return key. The number of the current line will be changed to the specified line number, and the contents of that line will be displayed on the screen. If a line number greater than the total number of lines is entered, the screen will display the following error message:

?

line out of range

For example, the following command:

10

would cause the current line number to be changed to line 10. Also, the contents of line 10 would be displayed on the screen.

MOVING TO THE LAST LINE

The last line in the buffer can be accessed without knowing the last line number. A dollar sign is used to represent the last line number. Typing a dollar sign and pressing the Return key will cause the current line number to be changed to the last line in the buffer. Also, the contents of the last line will be displayed on the screen. The number of the last line can be displayed on the screen by typing an equal sign and pressing the Return key.

For example, the following command:

=

would cause the value of the last line number in the file to be displayed on the screen. And, the command:

$

would cause the current line number to be changed to that of the last line in the file.

MOVING BY A SPECIFIC NUMBER OF LINES

The + and - commands are used to move the current line number a specific number of lines up or down in the buffer. The + command moves the current line closer to the end of the file. The - command moves the current line closer to the beginning of the file. The form of the + and - commands is as follows:

+number
or *-number*

where *number* represents the number of lines the current line is to be changed by. Both the + and - commands also cause the new current line to be displayed on the screen.

If the + command causes the line number to become larger than the last number or the - command causes the line number to become less than one, the following error message will be displayed on the screen:

?

line out of range

For example, the following command:

+5

would cause the current line to be changed to the line five lines forward in the file. If the current line was originally line 22, the command given above would cause the current line to be changed to line 27. Similarly the following command:

-7

would cause the current line to be changed to the line seven lines backwards in the file. If the current line was originally line 30, the command given above would cause the current line to be changed to line 23.

Displaying the File

The print command is used to display the file currently located in the editing buffer. The most useful form of the print command is:

*first line,lastline***p**

where *first line* represents the line number of the first line to be displayed and *last line* represents the line number of the last line to be displayed. The **p** is the print command. All lines between the first line and the last line will be displayed. The value of *first line* must be less than the value of *last line* for the command to work. Also, the current line number is changed to the number of the *last line*. An especially useful version of this command is:

1,$p

This command will cause the entire contents of the editing buffer to be displayed on the screen. Another example of the print command follows:

-2,+1p

This command would cause the following four lines to be displayed on the screen:

- The two lines prior to the current line
- The current line
- The line following the current line

Adding Lines to a File

Lines can be added to a file by either appending them after the current line or by inserting them before the current line. The simplest manner in which to use these two commands is to first locate the current line at the appropriate position in the file. Then the append or insert commands may be issued to add the necessary lines.

APPENDING

The append command adds lines to a file after the current line. Any lines that were in the file after the current line are moved down so that the new material is sandwiched between the old material. To start appending lines to a file, type **a** and press the Return key. The cursor will be moved to the beginning of the next line on the screen. Type the material to be appended. Pressing the Return key will begin a new line. To stop appending material to the file, type a period (.) by itself at the start of a new line and press the Return key. The current line will be set to the last appended line.

For example, the following sequence:

```
a
We are adding two lines. This is the first.
And, this is the second.

.
```

would cause the two lines of text to be placed into the file immediately after the current line. Suppose the file originally read:

```
This is the current line.
This is the line following the current line.
```

After the above append command was executed, the file would read:

```
This is the current line.
We are adding two lines. This is the first.
And this is the second.
This is the line following the current line.
```

Note that the current line would actually be set to the last line that was appended to the file. In this case, the current line would read:

```
And this is the second.
```

INSERTING

The insert command functions in a fashion identical to the append command except that the new material is inserted before the current line instead of after. To start inserting lines into a file, type **i** and press the Return key. The cursor will be moved to the beginning of the next line on the screen. Now, text is added as it was with the append command. The lone period will once again signal the end of additional material.

For example, the following sequence:

```
i
We are inserting two lines. This is the first.
And, this is the second.
.
```

would cause the two lines of text to be inserted into the file immediately before the current line. Suppose the file originally read:

```
This is the line before the current line.
This is the current line.
```

After the above insert command was executed, the file would read:

```
This is the line before the current line.
We are inserting two lines.
This is the first. And, this is the second.
This is the current line.
```

Note that the current line would actually be set to the last line that was inserted into the files. In this case, the current line would read:

```
And this is the second.
```

Deleting Lines from a File

The delete command is used to remove unwanted lines from the file. The delete command works in a manner similar to the print command. Typing **d** and pressing the Return key causes the current line to be removed. The command to remove more than one line has the form:

*first line,last line***d**

where *first line* represents the line number of the first line to be deleted and *last line* represents the number of the last line to be deleted. All lines between the first and the last line will also be deleted. The value of *first line* must be less than the value of *last line* in order for this command to work.

For example, the following command:

d

causes the current line to be deleted. The current line number will be changed to that of the next line in the file. When the last line in the file is deleted, the current line is changed to the previous line, which is the new last line. Also, the following command:

-6,+3d

would cause ten lines to be deleted. The current line, the six lines before the current line, and the three lines after the current line would be deleted.

Replacing Lines of a File

The change command is used to replace lines of a file with new lines of text. The action this command performs is equivalent to deleting the lines to be replaced and inserting the new lines of text.

The command to replace only one line of the file has the form:

line number c

where *line number* represents the line to be replaced. After the Return key is pressed to execute this command, the cursor will be located at the beginning of the next line. As many lines as necessary can be added by typing the text as with an append command. Pressing the Return key accesses a new line. A lone period at the beginning of a line signals that no more lines need be added. Note that one line can be replaced by several lines.

The command to replace several lines of the file has the form:

*first line,last line*c

where *first line* represents the number of the first line to be replaced and *last line* represents the number of the last line to be replaced. All lines between the first line and the last line are also replaced. After the Return key is pressed to execute this command, the new lines that are to replace the specified lines are entered as in the command to replace only one line.

For example, the following sequence:

```
-1,2c
Replace four lines with this one line.
.
```

would cause the current line, the line before the current line and the two lines after the current line to be changed to the single line of text. Suppose the file originally read:

```
This will stand.
Some line.
This is the current line.
Some line.
Some line.
This will stand, too.
```

After the preceding change command was executed, the file would read:

```
This will stand.
Replace four lines with this one line.
This will stand, too.
```

Note that the current line number would be set to that of the last line changed. In this case, the current line would read:

```
Replace four lines with one line.
```

Rearranging Lines Within a File

There are two methods of moving lines within the file being edited. The lines can be actually moved to a new location, or a copy of the lines can be transferred to the new location while they also remain at the original location.

MARKING A LINE

The move and transfer commands each require three different lines to be addressed. The simplest procedure to handle all the addresses is to mark the appropriate lines. The lines can then be referred to by the mark instead of by line number. The command to mark a line has the following format:

linekcharacter

where *line* represents the line number of the line to be marked and *character* represents the lowercase letter that will mark the line. The marked line can then be referred to by the following:

'character

where *character* represents the lowercase letter that was used to mark the line.

For example, the following command:

ka

would cause the current line to be marked with an **a**. The marked line can now be referred to by 'a instead of a line number.

MOVING LINES

The move command causes the specified lines to be moved from their present position to a new location. The move command has the following form:

*first line,last line**m**new line*

where *first line* represents the line number of the first line in the group of lines to be moved, *last line* represents the line number of the last line in the group of lines to be moved, and *new line* represents the line number of the line after which the lines being moved will be inserted.

For example, suppose we have the following file in the editing buffer:

```
one
two
three
four
five
six
seven
eight
nine
ten
eleven
twelve
```

Also suppose we want to move the following lines:

        two
        three
        four

so that they appear after the line depicted below:

        eleven

First, we will mark the necessary lines. We will then use the marked lines to specify the line numbers in the move command. The following table lists the necessary commands with a short explanation of their purpose:

Command	Purpose
2kb	Mark the line containing "two" with the letter "b".
4ke	Mark the line containing "four" with the letter "e".
11kr	Mark the line containing "eleven" with the letter "r".
'b,'em'r	Move the lines containing "two", "three", and "four" between the lines containing "eleven" and "twelve".

After typing the commands in the above table, the resulting file would appear as follows:

        one
        five
        six
        seven
        eight
        nine
        ten
        eleven
        two
        three
        four
        twelve

In a longer file where the line number cannot be easily determined, the necessary lines can be marked by first moving to the line of interest by using the + and - commands. The marks can then be made using the current line as the default for the line number in the mark command.

TRANSFERRING LINES

The transfer command causes the indicated lines to be copied at a specific location. The lines that were copied will appear at their current location as well as the new one. The transfer command has the following form:

*first line,last line*t*new line*

where *first line* represents the line number of the first line in the group of lines to be transferred, *last line* represents the line number of the last line in the group of lines to be transferred, and *new line* represents the line number of the line after which the lines being transferred will be inserted.

For example, suppose we wanted to accomplish the same task as with the example for the move command, except as a transfer. The file would be marked in the same manner. In place of the move command, we would issue the following transfer command:

'b,'et'r

As a result of this command, the file would appear as follows:

```
one
two
three
four
five
six
seven
eight
```
continued on following page

```
nine
ten
eleven
two
three
four
twelve
```

Note the difference in the results of the two commands.

JOINING TWO LINES

Contiguous lines may be joined to form one line. The join command has the following form:

*first line,last line*j

where *first line* represents the line number of the first line to be joined and *last line* represents the line number of the last line to be joined.

For example, suppose we have a file that contains the following lines:

```
one
two
three
```

Issuing the following command:

1,3j

will cause the file to be changed to the following:

onetwothree

Note that no space was provided for between the joined lines. We will discuss how to remedy this problem later.

Substitutions Within the Current Line

The substitute command allows an individual character or a string of characters to be changed within a line. The command to accomplish this task has the following form:

s/*search string*/*replacement string*/

where *search string* represents the character string to be replaced and *replacement string* represents the replacement character string.

For example, if the current line contained the following:

Lead is a precious metal.

issuing the following command:

s/Lead/Gold/p

would cause the line to be changed and displayed on the screen as follows:

Gold is a precious metal.

Note that a **p** included after the final slash causes the updated version of the line to be displayed on the screen.

Be sure to read the next section, which discusses special characters, before using the substitute command extensively. The special characters provide easier methods for accomplishing some tasks.

Special Characters

Before we can fully explain the use of commands that search the file for a piece of text, we must first discuss a few special characters. These characters carry a special meaning to the line editor program. We do not consider commands typed at the asterisk prompt to be special characters. The following characters can carry a special meaning:

^	the caret
$	the dollar sign
*	the asterisk (or star)
.	the period
/	the slash
\	the backslash
[	the left square bracket
]	the right square bracket

The context in which these characters are used can change their meaning. We will discuss the special characters in detail in the following sections.

THE CARET (^)

The caret is used to represent the beginning of the line. The caret is interpreted in this fashion only when it is the first character of a search string.

For example, if the current line contained the following,

Improved Potato Chips

the following command,

s/ ^/New, /p

would cause the line to be changed and displayed on the screen as follows:

New, Improved Potato Chips

Note that the caret has no special meaning when it is in the replacement string. If the current line is the line shown above, the following command illustrates this fact:

s/l/^/p

This command would cause the current line to be changed and displayed as follows:

New, ^mproved Potato Chips

Also, the caret has no special meaning if it is included somewhere other than at the start of the search string. If the current line is the one shown above, the following command illustrates this fact:

s/w, ^/w, l/p

This command would cause the current line to be changed and displayed as follows:

New, Improved Potato Chips

THE DOLLAR SIGN ($)

The dollar sign is used to represent the end of the line when it is used at the end of a search string. Do not confuse this application of the dollar sign with its usage to represent the last line of a file.

If the current line contained the following:

New, Improved Potato Chips

The following command:

s/$/ with Ridges/p

would cause the line to be changed and displayed on the screen as follows:

New, Improved Potato Chips with Ridges

As with the caret, the occurrence of a dollar sign in a replacement string or in some position of the search string other than last will have no special meaning.

THE PERIOD (.)

The utility of the period used as a special character is best demonstrated with a search for multiple items.

For example, if the current line contained the following:

New, Improved Potato Chips with Ridges

the following command:

s/,.*with//p

would replace everything from the comma to the word "with" by an empty replacement string. The **p** would cause the changed line to be displayed on the screen as follows:

New Ridges

A period is used to represent any single character in a search string. By any single character, we mean that the character in the position corresponding to the period can have any value and a match will still be found if the other characters correlate.

THE ASTERISK (*)

The asterisk is used to represent as many consecutive reoccurrences of the preceding character as possible. The asterisk can be used to locate and eliminate unnecessary repetitions of a character. Note carefully that the asterisk will match zero or more occurrences of the preceding character.

For example, suppose the following line is the current line:

Then, we   started to

The following command:

s/we   *started/we started/p

would cause the line to be changed and displayed on the screen as follows:

Then, we started to

THE SLASH (/)

The slash is used in substitute commands as the delimiter for search and character strings. The first slash signifies the beginning of the search string. The second slash signifies the end of the search string and the beginning of the replacement string. The third slash signals the end of the replacement string.

THE BACKSLASH (\ )

The backslash is used to defeat the special meaning of a special character. The backslash is used before a special character if the ordinary character is needed.

For example, suppose the current line contains the following:

The / and * are special characters.

The following command:

s/\ /   and */slash and asterisk/p

would cause the current line to be changed and displayed on the screen as follows:

The slash and asterisk are special characters.

THE LEFT ([) AND RIGHT (]) SQUARE BRACKETS

The left and right square brackets are used in search strings to delimit a choice of characters that will match a single character.

For example, the command:

s/[Uu] [Nn] [Ii] [Xx] /UNIX/p

would match Unix or unix or uNiX and change it to UNIX.

The square brackets are most useful in multiple line sustitutions, searchs, and search-and-edit commands. All of these are described in the following sections.

Repeated Substitution Within Lines

Up to now, all substitution commands that have been described only operate on the first occurrence of the search string that is found within the line. If the same substitution must be made more than once within a line, the global suffix to the substitute command is used. The substitute command with global suffix has the following form:

s/search string/replacement string/gp

Note that both the **g** and **p** suffixes are optional. The **g** causes the change to be made for every occurrence of the search string. The **p** causes the result to be printed on the screen.

Substitutions on Multiple Lines

If the same substitution must be made in several lines, the multiple line form of the substitute command is used. The multiple line substitute has the following form:

*first line,last lines/search string/replacement string/***gp**

where *first line, last line, search string,* and *replacement string,* and **s** retain the same meaning as in the regular substitute command. The specified substitution is performed on every line in the range from *first line* to *last line.* The **g** and **p** are each optional, as with the single line substitute command.

Recall the example where we joined several lines into one line (*see* page 89). The resulting line's words all ran together. To insert the correct spaces, we could have used the multiple line substitute command before joining the lines together. We need to add a space at the beginning of each of the lines that are to be joined to the first. Suppose that we are starting with the original file:

```
one
two
three
```

To insert the necessary spaces, the following command is used:

2,$s/ ^/ /

The result of joining all of the lines in the file would now be:

```
one two three
```

Searching a File

Files can be searched for the occurrence of a particular character key. The **ed** utility provides several commands for searching. The search can be conducted on a seek only basis, seek and edit basis or interactive seek and edit.

FORWARD SEARCH

A forward search scans forward in the file until the first match of the search string is found. The search will automatically wrap around from the end of the file to the beginning. The search will then be carried to the starting point, which is the current line. If the search is unsuccessful, the following message is displayed on the screen:

```
?
search string not found
```

If the search is successful, the current line is changed to the line number that contains the match, and that line is displayed on the screen. The command to accomplish a forward search has the following form:

/search string/

where *search string* is the character string being sought.

BACKWARD SEARCH

The backward search functions identically to the forward search except that the file is scanned in reverse. The wraparound, if it is necessary, will be from the beginning of the file to the end of the file. The command to initiate a backward search has the following form:

?search string?

where *search string* represents the character string being sought. On small files, it makes little difference whether the search is conducted forward or backward. On large files, search time can be reduced if it is known where in relation to the current line the line being sought is located.

SEARCH USED AS A LINE NUMBER

Forward and backward search can be used anywhere a line number would normally be used. Forward and backward search can be used in this manner to perform complex editing tasks. Examine the following multiple-line substitute command:

$$? \wedge BEGIN?+,/\wedge END/-s/\wedge / \ /$$

This command would cause the editor to search backward from the current line to a line containing the string **BEGIN** at the beginning of the line, and then search forward to a line containing **END** at the beginning of the line. The + and - cause the substitution to be performed on all lines from the line after the **BEGIN** to the line before the **END**. In this example, space would be inserted at the beginning of each line.

SEARCH AND EDIT

If it is known that each occurrence of a character string must be edited in an identical fashion, then the search and edit command can be used. The search and edit command searches a specified group of lines. Each occurrence of the search string is first found, and one after another, the current line is set to the line containing the match and the editing commands in the command list are executed. The search and edit command has the following form:

> *first line,last line***g***/search string/command* \
> *command* \
> *command*

where *first line* represents the line number the search will start at, *last line* represents the line number the search will end at, *search string* represents the character string being sought and each occurrence of *command* represents an editing command that is to be carried out. These commands comprise the command list. Note that the backslash is used to indicate that there is another command in the list. If only one command is to be executed for each search string found, no backslash is needed.

Suppose a text file had been labeled with "NEEDS INFO" each time an unavailable piece of data was referenced by the text. When that piece of data became available, it could be inserted into the text using the following search and edit command:

```
g/NEEDS INFO/s/NEEDS INFO/HEADER/ \
a \
text \
text \
.
```

This command would cause each occurrence of "NEEDS INFO" to be changed to "HEADER." It would also insert the two lines of text after the header. Note that when the lines to be searched are not specified, the search and edit command acts upon the entire file.

Be careful of the distinction between the **g** *command*, for global search and edit, and the **g** *suffix* for global replacement within a single line.

INVERSE SEARCH AND EDIT

The inverse search and edit command is identical to the search and edit command except that lines that do not contain a match to the search string are acted upon. The inverse search and edit command has the following form:

```
first line,last linev/search string/command \
command \
command
```

where *first line, last line, search string,* and *command* have the same meaning as in the search and edit command.

INTERACTIVE SEARCH AND EDIT

The interactive search and edit command marks each occurrence of the search string that is found in the specified group of lines. Then, the first marked line is displayed on the screen. The value of the current line is set to that line. One editing command can be executed in that line. Pressing the Return key causes a null command to be executed. After a command is executed, the next marked line is displayed. After the last marked line has been dealt with, the asterisk prompt returns to the screen.

The interactive search and edit command has the following form:

*first line,last line***G**/*search string*/

where *first line* represents the line number at which the search is to start, *last line* represents the line number at which the search is to end, and *search string* represents the character string being sought. Note that if no line numbers are specified, the interactive search and edit command will act upon the entire file.

INVERSE INTERACTIVE SEARCH AND EDIT

The inverse interactive search and edit command is identical to the interactive search and edit command except the lines that do not contain a match to the search string are acted upon. The inverse interactive search and edit has the following form:

*first line,last line***V**/*search string*/

where *first line, last line,* and *search string* have the same meaning as in the interactive search and edit command.

Bringing Files into the Editing Buffer

Files from the UNIX file system can be brought into the editing buffer. These files can either be added to the file presently in the buffer, or they can replace that file.

READ

The read command is used to add a file to the file currently in the editing buffer. The read command has the following form:

liner filename

where *line* represents the line number after which the new file should be placed and *filename* represents the UNIX file that is to be added to the editing buffer. If *line* is omitted, the new file will be placed immediately after the file currently in the editing buffer.

For example, the following command:

15r table

would cause the file **table** to be inserted into the file presently in the buffer. The file, **table,** would be inserted after line 15 but before line 16.

EDIT

The edit command is used to start editing a new file. If changes made on the current file in the editing buffer have not been saved, the following warning will appear on the screen:

```
?
warning: expecting 'w'
```

A second edit command will cause the new file to be moved into the editing buffer without saving the present contents of the buffer.

The edit command has the following form:

e *filename*

where *filename* represents the name of the UNIX file to be updated. For example, the following command:

e memo

would cause the file **memo** to replace the current contents of the editing buffer and the current filename to be changed to **memo**.

Undoing Editing Errors

The undo command allows the last change made on the editing buffer to be undone. Specifically, the undo command reverses the effect of the most recently executed command from the following list:

- append (**a**)
- change (**c**)
- delete (**d**)
- search and edit (**g**)
- inverse search and edit (**v**)
- interactive search and edit (**G**)
- inverse interactive search and edit (**V**)
- insert (**i**)
- join (**j**)
- move (**m**)
- read (**r**)
- substitute (**s**)
- transfer (**t**)
- undo (**u**)

The undo command has the following form:

u

By checking the result of each editing command and undoing mistakes, much time can be saved. The results from commands that affect many lines, such as the search and edit commands, should be checked with particular care.

Running Shell Commands from ed

Shell commands can be run without exiting from **ed.** This facility can be useful to find and view files to add to the editing buffer. The command to run a shell command from the **ed** utility has the following form:

!*shell command*

where *shell command* represents the UNIX shell command to run.

For example, the following command:

!ls

would send the command **ls** to the shell, which would then cause the contents of the current working directory to be displayed. And, the following command:

!cat table

would execute the shell command **cat**, and cause the contents of the file **table** to be displayed on the screen.

Summary

Table 4.1 summarizes the **ed** commands. Note that we did not discuss a few of the listed commands. These commands were included in the table for the sake of completeness. The commands that we did not cover will be of interest only for special applications. For more information on these commands, refer to the system documentation.

Table 4.1. Summary of **ed** commands

Command Name	Command Format	Description	Page
append	**a** *text* .	Appends text after current line.	80
change	*line, line* **c** *text* .	Changes specified lines to the given text.	84
delete	*line, line* **d**	Deletes the specified lines	83
edit	**e** *filename*	Edit a different file.	101
file	**f** *filename*	Changes the currently specified file.	76
search and edit	**g**/*search string*/ *command list*	Executes commands starting at the lines that contain the search string.	98
interactive search and edit	**G**/*search string*/	Finds each occurrence of search string and allows manual editing on each.	100
help	**h**	Provides explanation of errors.	76
	H	Turns on and off error messages.	75
insert	**i** *text*	Inserts text before the current line.	82

continued on following page

Table 4.1. (cont.) Summary of **ed** commands

Command Name	Command Format	Description	Page
inverse search and edit	**v**/*search string*/ *command list*	Executes the command string starting at lines that do not contain the search string.	99
inverse interactive search and edit	**V**/*search string*	Finds each line that does not contain the search string and allows manual editing on each.	100
join	*line, line* **j**	Joins specified lines.	89
mark	*line* **k** *character*	Marks specified line with specified character.	85
list	*line,line***l**	Lists specified lines; includes unprintable characters.	--
move	*line,line***m***line*	Moves specified line to new location.	86
number	*line,line***n**	Displays specified lines, preceded by their line number.	--
print	*line,line***p**	Displays specified lines.	99
prompt	**P**	Causes asterisk prompt to be displayed/not displayed.	--
quit	**q**	Causes exit from **ed**. Checks if write has been done.	75
	Q	Causes exit from ed. Does not check if write has been done. Same as a two **q** commands.	
read	*line* **r** *file name*	Reads specified file into the editing buffer after the specified line number.	101
substitute	*line,line* **s** /*search string*/ *replacement string*/**gp**	Searches specified *lines* for the first occurrence of the search string and replaces it with the replacement string. **g** causes multiple substitution within a line. **p** causes the resulting line to be displayed.	90

continued on following page

Table 4.1. (cont.) Summary of **ed** commands

Command Name	Command Format	Description	Page
transfer	*line,line*t*line*	Transfers a copy of the specified lines to the specified location. Leaves the original location unaltered.	86
undo	u	Undoes the effect of the last command that modified the editing buffer (i.e., a, c, d, g, i, j, m, r, s, t, v, G, or V).	102
write	w	Writes the buffer to the current filename.	76
	*line,line*w *filename*	Writes the specified lines to the specified file.	
	*line,line*w>> *filename*	Appends the specified lines to the end of the specified file.	
use **crypt** with **ed**	X	Uses the **crypt** utility when reading and writing files.	--
display line	=	Displays the number of last line.	78
number	.=	Displays the line number of the current line.	77
shell command	! *command*	Runs a shell command from **ed**.	103
change current line number	$command	Changes the current line number to that of the file's last line	78
move up or down	+ -	+ moves the current line closer to the end of the file by the number of lines specified; - moves the current line toward the beginning of the file.	78

vi — A SCREEN EDITOR

Any text file can be created and edited using the **vi** utility. The **vi** utility is a full screen editor. A full screen editor allows the user to view and modify text displayed on the entire terminal screen. Generally, one screen contains approximately 25 lines. If the entire file will not fit on the screen, only a portion of the file is displayed. The other portions of the file can be viewed with the scrolling commands.

The screen editor allows the user to position the cursor at any point on the screen. Screen oriented editing commands generally affect the file at the point where the cursor is positioned. In addition to the screen oriented commands, **vi** also provides line oriented commands. These commands generally affect the current line of the file. The current line is the line that presently contains the cursor.

In this section, we will discuss both the screen and line oriented commands. In addition, we cover how to enter and exit the **vi** utility and how to move the cursor.

Entering vi

The **vi** utility can be invoked in several different manners. How the utility is invoked depends upon the task at hand.

SIMPLEST METHOD

The easiest method of invoking the screen editor utility from the UNIX shell is to simply type **vi** and press the Return key. When the **vi** utility is invoked in this fashion, the screen editor is opened but no particular file is specified. New text can now be created and modified. When the editor is exited, a file to write to must be specified in order to save the text created during the editing session.

The screen will appear as follows:

```
[ ]
~
~
~
~
~
~
~
```

Note that each tilde represents a potential line. A potential line is only a place holder on the screen and will not appear in the file. A potential line becomes an actual line when text or a carriage return is added to it. We represented only a few of the potential lines. In reality, the potential lines would fill the screen. We use the pair of square brackets to represent the position of the cursor.

WITH A FILE SPECIFIED

A more useful method of entering the **vi** utility is to open the editor and specify the file to edit at the same time. The command to accomplish this task has the following form:

vi *filename*

where *filename* represents the name of the file to be edited. If that file already exists, it will be loaded into the editing buffer and the text, beginning at the first line, will be displayed on the screen.

The concept of the editing buffer is important to understand. The editor does not act directly on the specified file. Instead, a copy of the file is placed in the editing buffer. All changes made during the editing session are made on the copy of the specified file. The file itself is not changed until a write command is issued. A write command causes the contents of the editing buffer to overwrite the contents of the specified file.

For example, to enter the screen editor with the file **tryit** specified, the following command would be used:

vi tryit

As a result of this command, the file **tryit** would be loaded into the editing buffer and the **vi** utility would be entered. The screen display might resemble the following:

```
[T]his is a practice file.
Presently it ony has a few lines.
~
~
~
~
~
~
"tryit" 2 lines, 60 characters
```

Note that we only represented a few of the potential lines, which are marked by the tildes. The present position of the cursor is on the first letter in the file, which is a "T". In this book the position of the cursor is indicated by the square brackets that enclose the "T". The last line of the display is the status line. The status line provides information about the specified file. We will see later that the status line is also used to display line oriented and other special commands.

One important case to consider is when a nonexistent file is specified as the file to edit. Suppose the file **empty** does not exist. The following command:

vi empty

would result in the following screen display:

```
[ ]
~
~
~
~
"empty" No such file or directory
```

The file **empty** does not presently exist in the user's search path. The file will not be created until it is written from the **vi** utility. Note that the file will not be created if text is not added to the editing buffer before the quit command is issued. Specifying a file that does not exist is a convenient method of creating a new file. If a write command is issued before any text is added, a file containing a single empty line will be created.

STARTING AT A SPECIFIED LINE WITHIN THE FILE

The **vi** utility may also be invoked so that the cursor is placed at a location other than the beginning of the first line of the specified file. There are three basic variations in this method of entering **vi.**

The most useful is the command to place the cursor at the beginning of the last line of the file. This command has the following form:

vi + *filename*

where *filename* represents the name of the specified file.

Another method of invoking the **vi** utility allows a specific line number to be indicated. The cursor will be placed at the beginning of the specified line number. This command has the following form:

vi +*line number   filename*

where *line number* represents the number of the line in which the cursor is to be placed, and *filename* represents the name of the file to be edited. Note that in the first form the **+** is typed as a word by itself, and in the second form, the **+line number** is also typed as one word.

Finally, the occurrence of a specific string can be searched for. The cursor will be placed at the beginning of the line that contains the specified string. This command has the following form:

vi +/*search string   filename*

where *search string* represents the specified string and *filename* represents the name of the file to be edited. If the search string contains spaces, the entire string must be enclosed in quotes (″) to avoid having parts of the string interpreted as filenames. Note that if the search string is not found, the cursor will be placed at the beginning of the last line in the file.

RECOVERING AN UNSAVED FILE AFTER A SYSTEM CRASH

If the system crashes while a file is being edited, the changes made during the editing session are not necessarily lost. The **vi** utility can be invoked in a special fashion in order to attempt to recover the file. This command has the following form:

vi -r *filename*

where *filename* represents the name of the file that was being edited at the time of the system crash, and **-r** indicates the recover option of **vi**.

Even with the above safety feature, it is a good practice to periodically write the file being edited. This action provides insurance from inadvertent destruction of the file in the editing buffer.

Modes

The **vi** utility has different modes of operation. The mode determines how input from the keyboard is interpreted. The **vi** utility has three different modes. Command mode is active when **vi** is first invoked. Either of the other modes may be entered from command mode, and will return to command mode when they are exited.

COMMAND MODE

The **vi** utility is placed in the command mode on being invoked. In the command mode, any input from the keyboard is interpreted as an editing command. If the computer's speaker sounds when the Escape key is depressed, then the command mode is active. The command mode can be made active by holding the Escape key in the depressed position until the speaker sounds. While in the command mode, depressing a key that is not defined as part of an editing command will cause the speaker to sound. Note that the commands are never displayed on the screen. All of these commands are very short. Their input causes an immediate action.

INSERT MODE

In the insert mode, any input from the keyboard is placed into the editing buffer. The insert mode is used to create new text within the file. The insert mode can be activated by any of the following **vi** editing commands: insert, append, open, substitute, change, or replace (**i, I, a, A, o, O, s, S, c, C, r, R**). The insert mode is exited by pressing the Escape key.

ESCAPE MODE

In the escape mode, input from the keyboard is interpreted as a special command. These special commands allow file manipulation and the use of line oriented editing commands. Generally, these commands start with a colon (:) and are terminated by a carriage return. The text of these commands will appear on the status line. Recall that the status line is the bottom line of the screen display. Note that the status line is also used by the slash (/) command from command mode. Do not confuse this use of the status line with the escape mode.

Exiting vi

The changes made to a file are usually saved before the **vi** utility is exited. However, it is possible to quit the editor without saving the contents of the file. The **vi** utility can be temporarily exited to execute shell commands. After the necessary shell commands have been completed, control is returned to the **vi** utility. It is also possible to write a file without quitting the editor. Commands to exit the **vi** screen editor are available in both the command mode and the escape mode.

EXITING AND SAVING

The command most often used to quit the screen editor causes the contents of the editing buffer to overwrite the specified file before exiting the **vi** utility. The specified file is the file that was named when **vi** was invoked unless a different file is specified in the quit command.

The command to write to the currently specified file and quit the screen editor has the following two forms:

ZZ
or
:x

In the case of the **:x** command, **vi** will change to the escape mode. The colon and the "x" will be displayed on the status line. In both cases, the status line will display the name of the file being written to, the number of lines in the file and the number of characters in the file. After this information is displayed, the shell prompt will appear on the screen, indicating that **vi** is closed.

The command to write to a file other than the currently specified file and exit the screen editor has the following form:

:x *filename*

where *filename* is the name of the file to be written to. This command is useful if the contents of the original file should not be overwritten. For example, typing the following from the command mode of **vi:**

:x newfile

and pressing the Return key would cause the current contents of the editing buffer to be stored in the file **newfile.** Note that the original file would not be altered. If **newfile** already existed, it would be overwritten. If **newfile** did not previously exist, it would be created in the current working directory.

vi can also be exited by pressing the Escape key followed by **ZZ.**

SAVING WITHOUT EDITING

In some cases it may be desirable to write to a file without exiting the **vi** utility. Either the currently specified file or a different file can be written to. One reason to write to a file without exiting **vi** is to save all the previous editing changes during a long editing session as a precautionary measure.

The command to write to a file without quitting the screen editor has the following form:

:w *filename*

where *filename* is the name of the file to be written to. If *filename* is omitted, the currently specified file will be written to. Note that specifying *filename* affects only this particular write command. The currently specified file is not changed.

This means that if the file **original** is the currently specified file, the following command:

:w newfile

would cause the file **newfile** to be created. But, if the following command was then issued:

:x

the file **original** would be overwritten with the contents of the editing buffer.

For details on how to change the name of the currently specified file, refer to the section on "Saving Edited Files" in the **ed** part of this chapter (page 76). Nearly all **ed** commands are available in escape mode. For more information, see the section on line oriented commands near the end of this chapter (page 134).

EXITING WITHOUT SAVING

If for some reason it is decided that the contents of the editing buffer are not useful, **vi** can be exited without saving the buffer. Once such an action is taken, the contents of that buffer are irretrievably lost.

If the currently specified file exists, it will remain as it was as of the beginning of the editing session or the last write command. If the specified file does not already exist, it will not be created.

The command to quit the screen editor without saving the contents of the editing buffer has the following form:

:q!

Use this command with care. Be sure the contents of the editing buffer are unnecessary before issuing the command.

EDITING ANOTHER FILE

If the editing tasks on one file are completed but another file also must be edited, the next file can be called into the editing buffer. The current contents of the editing buffer should first be saved using a **:w** command.

The command to replace the current contents of the editing buffer with another file has the following form:

:e *filename*

where *filename* represents the name of the file to be placed in the buffer. If the current contents of the editing buffer have not been saved, the following message will appear on the status line:

No write since last change (:edit!overrides)

As the message states, the following command will allow another file to be placed in the editing buffer without saving the current contents of the buffer:

:e! *filename*

where *filename* is the name of the file to be placed in the editing buffer.

EXECUTING A SHELL COMMAND

It is possible to execute a shell command without leaving the **vi** utility. The command to accomplish this task has the following form:

:!*shell command*

where *shell command* represents any valid UNIX shell command. For example, typing:

:!cat results

would cause the **cat** command to display the **results** file on the screen. At the end of the display, the following message will be displayed:

[Hit return to continue]

Pressing the Return key will cause the screen to be redrawn. The new display will exhibit the same information that appeared on the screen before the shell command was executed.

Scrolling

Scrolling is used to access part of the file that is not presently displayed on the screen. The **vi** editor allows for both forward and backward scrolling by increments of either a full screen or a half screen. A scroll always accesses contiguous lines in the file. A forward scroll, sometimes called "scrolling down", always moves the display toward the end of the file. A backward scroll, sometimes called "scrolling up", always moves the display toward the beginning of the file. The scroll commands only function in the command mode.

FORWARD

The control-d combination causes a scroll of one-half screen forward in the file. The control-f combination causes a scroll of a full screen forward in the file.

BACKWARD

The control-u combination causes a scroll of one-half screen backward in the file. The control-b combination causes a scroll of a full screen backward in the file.

Moving the Cursor

The cursor can be moved about within the file. If a command is issued that causes the cursor to be moved to a point that is not currently displayed on the screen, the screen display will be redrawn so that the cursor is included in the display.

Generally, if a number is input immediately before a command that causes a cursor movement, the cursor will be moved that number of spaces, lines, words, etc. Examples included with the discussion of the commands will help clarify this point. All cursor movement commands must be input while **vi** is in the command mode.

BY THE SPACE

The cursor can be moved by single spaces both to the right and the left. The commands that cause the cursor to be moved by single spaces will not move the cursor from its present line. If the command indicates that the cursor should be moved past the beginning or the end of the line, the cursor will be moved to the beginning or end of the line, respectively. The cursor will not be moved beyond the current line, nor will it wrap around to the next line.

Pressing the l key or the space bar causes the cursor to be moved one space to the right. To move six spaces to the right, type **6l**.

Pressing the **h** key or the backspace key (labelled ← on an IBM PC XT) causes the cursor to be moved one space to the left. To move nine spaces to the left, type **9h**.

TO THE BEGINNING OF THE CURRENT LINE

The cursor can be moved to the beginning of the current line. To accomplish this task, type **0**.

TO THE END OF THE CURRENT LINE

The cursor can be moved to the end of the current line by typing **$**.

TO A SPECIFIC COLUMN

The | command allows the cursor to be moved to any column in the current line. A column is a one character space in a line. Generally, terminal screens include 80 columns. To move to the fortieth column, type **40|**. The| command will not cause the cursor to move beyond the beginning or the end of the current line.

BY THE WORD

The cursor can either be moved forward (to the right) to the beginning of the next word or backward, to the beginning of the previous word. If the cursor is presently in the middle of a word, a command to move the cursor backward by one word will cause the cursor to be repositioned at the beginning of that word. For example, suppose the cursor were presently located at the indicated position:

wo[r]d

A command to move one word backward would cause the cursor to be repositioned so that it rested on the "w".

When counting words, punctuation can either be included or excluded from the word count. Which forms of the cursor movement by the word commands are used depends on personal preference and circumstances.

To move forward either the w or W keys are used. Pressing the w key causes the cursor to be moved one word to the right. Punctuation marks are counted as words. Pressing the W key causes the cursor to be moved one word to the right, where punctuation marks are not counted as words. Unlike moving the cursor by a single space, the command to move the cursor by the word will cause the cursor to wrap around to the next line. Finally, a command such as **7W** will cause the cursor to be moved forward to the beginning of the seventh word. The cursor will be moved forward as many lines as necessary to find the seventh word.

The b and B keys are used to move the cursor backward by words in the file. The b command is the counterpart to the w command while the B command is the counterpart to the W command.

The cursor can also be moved to the end of the next word forward in the file. The e and E keys are used in a fashion identical to the w and W keys, respectively. The cursor is placed at the end of the word instead of the beginning.

BY THE LINE

The cursor can be moved by the line both backward and forward in the file. The cursor can either be placed at the beginning of the line it was moved to or in the same column as it occupied in the line it was moved from.

The + and Return keys cause the cursor to be moved forward one line in the file and placed at the beginning of the line. The j and control-n keys cause the cursor to be moved forward one line while maintaining the cursor's column position.

To move the cursor several lines at once, type the desired number immediately before typing the command key. For example, typing **6+** will cause the cursor to be repositioned at the beginning of the sixth line forward in the file.

The k and control-p keys cause an identical action to the j and control-n keys except the cursor is moved backward in the file. The - key causes an identical action to the + and Return keys except the cursor is moved backward.

Inserting Text

Text can be inserted at any position in the file. The **vi** utility has several insertion commands. Each command starts inserting text at a slightly different point in the file. The actual point of insertion is determined in relation to the position of the cursor.

All of the insertion commands must be given while **vi** is in the command mode. All of these commands cause the mode to be changed to the insert mode. All characters input via the keyboard are placed into the editing buffer and displayed on the screen. These characters are placed at the position indicated by the cursor. Pressing the Return key is treated as a part of the text and will cause a new line to be accessed. The insert mode is exited by pressing the escape key after all necessary insertions have been completed. When the insert mode is exited, **vi** returns to the command mode.

BEFORE THE CURSOR

The **i** command is used to start insertion of text before the current position of the cursor. To initiate an **i** command, simply press the i key while **vi** is in the command mode. Recall that **vi** can be forced to the command mode by holding the Escape key down until the terminal speaker sounds.

The **i** command is quite often used to start inputting text into an empty editing buffer. As much text as is necessary can be added using **i** or any of the other insert commands.

For example, suppose the cursor was positioned on a line as shown below:

cur[s]or

where [ ] indicates the cursor. Issuing an i command, typing a 1 and a 2, and pressing the Escape key would cause the line to be changed as follows:

cur1[2]sor

BEFORE THE FIRST CHARACTER OF THE CURRENT LINE

The I command is used to start insertion of text before the first character in the current line. Recall that the current line is the line in which the cursor presently appears. To initiate an I command, press the I key while vi is in the command mode.

For example, suppose the cursor was positioned on a line as shown below:

cur[s]or

Issuing an I command, typing a 1 and a 2, and pressing the Escape key would cause the line to be changed as follows:

1[2]cursor

AFTER THE CURSOR

The a command is used to start insertion of text after the cursor. To initiate an a command, press the a key while vi is in the command mode.

For example, suppose the cursor was positioned on a line as shown below:

cur[s]or

Issuing an a command, typing a 1 and a 2, and pressing the Escape key would cause the line to be changed as follows:

curs1[2]or

AFTER THE LAST CHARACTER OF THE CURRENT LINE

The **A** command is used to start insertion of text after the last character of the current line. To initiate an **A** command, press the A key while **vi** is in the command mode.

For example, suppose the cursor was positioned on a line as shown below:

cur[s]or

Issuing an **A** command, typing a 1 and a 2, and pressing the Escape key would cause the line to be changed as follows:

cursor1[2]

AT THE BEGINNING OF A NEW LINE BELOW THE CURRENT LINE

The **o** command is used to start insertion of text at the beginning of a new line directly below the current line. To initiate an **o** command, press the o key while **vi** is in the command mode.

For example, suppose the cursor was positioned as shown below:

Line above the current line.
cur[s]or
Line below the current line.

Issuing an **o** command, typing a 1 and a 2, and pressing the Escape key would cause the display to be changed as follows:

Line above the current line.
cursor
1[2]
Line below the current line.

AT THE BEGINNING OF A NEW LINE ABOVE
THE CURRENT LINE

The **O** command is used to start insertion of text at the beginning of a new line directly above the current line. To initiate an **O** command, press the O key while **vi** is in the command mode.

For example, suppose the cursor was positioned as shown below:

```
Line above the current line.
cur[s]or
Line below the current line.
```

Issuing an **O** command, typing a 1 and a 2, and pressing the Escape key would cause the display to be changed as follows:

```
Line above the current line.
1[2]
cursor
Line below the current line.
```

Deleting Text

Text can be deleted at any position in the file. The **vi** utility has several deletion commands. Each command deletes a different amount of text or starts deleting the text from a different point in the file. Which part of the editing buffer is actually deleted is determined by the position of the cursor.

All of the deletion commands must be executed while **vi** is in the command mode. All of the commands cause the specified text to be removed from the editing buffer. The mode is never changed from the command mode.

DELETING CHARACTERS FORWARD

The x command is used to delete characters in the forward direction (to the right). The x command always starts deleting with the character underneath the cursor. More than one character can be deleted by specifying a number immediately before the x command. The x command has the following form:

number x

where *number* represents the number of characters to be deleted.

For example, suppose the cursor was positioned on a line as shown below:

```
cur[s]or
Line below the current line.
```

Issuing the following command,

2x

would cause the line to be changed as follows:

```
cur[r]
Line below the current line.
```

Note that the x command will only delete characters on the current line. So, if the following command had been issued in place of **2x**,

34x

the result would have been as follows:

```
cu[r]
Line below the current line.
```

DELETING CHARACTERS BACKWARD

The **X** command is used to delete characters in the backward direction (to the left). The **X** command always starts deleting with the first character to the left of the character the cursor is currently resting upon. More than one character can be deleted by specifying a number immediately before the **X** command. The **X** command has the following form:

*number***X**

where *number* represents the number of characters to be deleted.

For example, suppose the cursor was positioned on a line as shown below:

```
Line above the current line.
cur[s]or
```

Issuing the following command,

2X

would cause the line to be changed as follows:

```
Line above the current line.
c[s]or
```

Note that the **X** command will only delete characters on the current line. So, if the following command had been issued in place of **2X**,

34X

the result would have been as follows:

```
Line above the current line.
[s]or
```

DELETING WORDS

The **dw** command is used to delete words. If the cursor is located in the middle of a word, it will delete from the character underneath the cursor to the end of the word. If a number is specified immediately before the **dw** command, then that number of words will be deleted. Punctuation marks are counted as words. The **dw** command has the following form:

*number***dw**

where *number* represents the number of words to be deleted. For example, suppose the current line appears as follows:

```
The cur[s]or is in the current line.
The line following the current line.
```

The following command:

dw

would cause the following changes:

```
The cur[i]s in the current line.
The line following the current line.
```

Also, starting from the original configuration, the following command:

9dw

would cause the following changes:

```
The cur[f]ollowing the current line.
```

Note that the period was counted as a word. Also, a **dw** command can affect lines other than the current line. Finally, the **dw** command causes two lines to be joined when words are deleted from two or more lines by a single command. The **dW** command is identical to the **dw** command, except that punctuation marks are not counted as words.

DELETING FROM THE BEGINNING OF A LINE

The **d0** command is used to delete from the beginning of the line up to the character before the character beneath the cursor. The **d0** command has the following form:

d0

For example, suppose the current line appears as follows:

The cur[s]or in the current line.

Issuing the following command:

d0

would cause the following changes:

[s]or in the current line.

DELETING TO THE END OF A LINE

The **d$** command is used to delete from the character beneath the cursor to the end of the current line. The **d$** command has the following form:

d$

For example, suppose the current line appears as follows:

The cur[s]or in the current line.

Issuing the following command:

d$

would cause the following changes:

The cu[r]

DELETING FUTURE LINES

The **dd** command is used to delete the entire current line or a group of lines starting with the current line. The **dd** command has the following form:

*number***dd**

where *number* represents the number of lines to be deleted. For example, suppose part of a file appears as follows:

```
The curren[t] line
two
three
four
five
```

Issuing the following command:

dd

would cause the file to be changed as follows:

```
[t]wo
three
four
five
```

Also, starting with the original file, issuing the following command:

4dd

would cause the file to be changed as follows:

[f]ive

Substituting Text

A substitution accomplishes the action of a deletion of certain text and the insertion of other text. Varying amounts of text can be substituted for at any point in the editing buffer. The part of the file actually affected by a substitution is determined by the position of the cursor.

All of the substitution commands must be executed while **vi** is in the command mode. Generally, these commands cause **vi** to enter the insert mode. Recall that the insert mode is exited by pressing the Escape key.

REPLACE A SINGLE CHARACTER

The **r** command is used to replace a single character. The character the cursor is resting upon is changed to the character that is input immediately following the **r** command. The **r** command has the following form:

r

For example, suppose the current line appears as follows:

Current line contains an err[e]r.

The following command will correct the spelling error:

r

followed by typing an "o". The current line would appear as follows after the command shown above was executed:

Current line contains an err[o]r.

Note that this command does not cause the insert mode to be entered.

REPLACING MORE THAN ONE CHARACTER

The **R** command is used to replace more than one character. The replacement starts with the character beneath the cursor and proceeds to the right. The **R** command has the following form:

R

For example, suppose the current line appears as follows:

Current line contains [a]n error.

The following command:

R

followed by typing "no" and pressing the Escape key would cause the current line to appear as follows:

Current line contains n[o] error.

The **R** command will only overwrite characters through the end of the current line. More text and even additional lines may be typed and will be inserted, but no other text will be deleted.

CHANGING WORDS

The **cw** command is used to change one or more words. Punctuation marks are regarded as words. The replacement starts at the character beneath the cursor. The **cw** command has the following form:

*number***cw**

where *number* represents the number of words to be deleted.

For example, suppose the current line appears as follows:

The current line contains no [e]rrors.

Issuing the following command,

cw

typing "mistakes" and pressing the Escape key would cause the current line to appear as follows:

The current line contains no mistake[s].

Now, suppose the current line appears as follows:

The current line c[o]ntains no mistakes.

Issuing the following command:

3cw

typing "leaned up" and pressing the Return key would result in the current line appearing as:

The current line cleaned u[p].

The **cW** command is identical to the **cw** command, except that punctuation marks are not treated as words.

CHANGING LINES

The **cc** command is used to change the entire current line or a group of lines starting with the current line. The number of new lines inserted need not equal the number of old lines deleted. The **cc** command has the following form:

*number***cc**

where *number* represents the number of old lines to be deleted.

For example, suppose part of a file appears as follows:

```
The curren[t] line
two
three
four
five
```

The following command,

cc

typing "one" and pressing the Escape key would cause the file to appear as:

```
on[e]
two
three
four
five
```

Now, entering the following command,

3cc

typing,

```
The current line.
The line after the current line.
The third line.
```

and pressing the Escape key would cause the file to appear as:

```
The current line.
The line after the current line.
The third line[.]
four
five
```

CORRECTING EDITING MISTAKES

The **u** command is used to correct editing blunders. The **u** command undoes the last command that changed the contents of the editing buffer. If an editing command does not have the desired effect, it is often easiest to use the **u** command to undo the command. A different editing approach may then be attempted. The **u** command has the following form:

u

For example, if after the final example command in the previous section, a **u** command had been issued, the file would have been returned to the following state:

one
two
three
four
five

Note that only the last editing command was undone. Serious editing mistakes can be avoided by carefully examining the result of each editing command and undoing commands with undesirable effects.

The **u** command, if given a second time, will undo the previous **u** command, restoring the change.

LINE ORIENTED COMMANDS

Line oriented commands are available in **vi.** Line oriented commands are commands such as those found in the **ed** utility. Generally, the commands found in the **ed** utility are available in **vi.** To access an **ed** command from **vi,** first type a colon while **vi** is in the command mode. The colon will appear on the status line. **vi** will now be in escape mode. After the colon, type the desired **ed** command. Note that the only **ed** commands that may be used in the escape mode of **vi** are those that can be written on a single line. For more on line oriented commands, see the section on the line editor, presented earlier in this chapter.

Other vi Commands

There are a few other **vi** commands that are important in any introduction to this powerful screen editor.

REPEATING CHANGES

The period or dot command (.) will repeat the action of the previous change command. The last command is the same command that would be undone by the **u** command. Note that the dot command will not repeat the action of the **u** command. The dot command is most often used to make similar changes at several different places within a file. It may only be used from the command mode.

SEARCHING THE FILE

Search commands are available in the command mode of **vi**. A slash (/) begins the command to search forward and a question mark (?) begins the command to search backward. When typed, the slash or question mark will appear on the status line, and may be followed by the search string. For more on search strings and the special meanings of different characters, see the section on searching a file with the line editor, presented earlier in this chapter. Note that the slash or question mark is typed in command mode, not in escape mode.

Pressing the Return key marks the end of the search string and begins the search. The cursor will be placed on the first character of the string that is found.

The search may be repeated for the next occurrence of the search string, forward or backward as given, by using the **n** command. The search may be in the opposite direction by giving the **N** command. The **n** and **N** commands must be used from the command mode.

Summary

The following tables group the related **vi** commands. All of the commands that we discussed are listed in these tables. We have also included a few commands that we did not discuss. The individual user might find these useful in specific instances. For more information on these commands, consult the system documentation.

Finally, some of the commands of the **vi** program are not included. These commands embrace more advanced or more obscure topics and are beyond the scope of a simple introduction. Many of these commands deal with customizing the **vi** environment. The **vi** environment is changed by specifying options. The **vi** utility has approximately 40 environment options. These options typically deal with parameters such as whether or not error messages should be displayed on the screen and with features such as automatic indenting of lines. The **vi** utility works well using the default settings of these options. There are many additional editing commands, but in our opinion the majority of the important basic features of the **vi** utility were covered in this chapter.

Table 4.2. Commands used to enter the **vi** utility

Command Function	Command Form	Page
Invoke **vi** with no file to edit specified.	**vi**	107
Invoke **vi** with file specified.	**vi** *filename*	108
Invoke **vi** with file specified and position cursor at beginning of the last line in the file.	**vi** + *filename*	110
Invoke **vi** with file specified and position cursor at the beginning of the specified line.	**vi** +*line number filename*	110
Invoke **vi** with file specified and position cursor at the line containing the first occurrence of the search string.	**vi** +/*search string filename*	111
Invoke **vi** for an attempt to recover a file being edited when the system crashed.	**vi** -r *filename*	111

Table 4.3. Commands used to save the editing buffer and exit the **vi** utility.

Command Function	Command Form	Page
Write contents of the editing buffer to the currently specified file and exit the the screen editor.	**ZZ** or **:x**	113
Write contents of the editing buffer to a file other than the currently specified file and exit **vi**.	**:x** *filename*	113
Write contents of the editing buffer to the specified file. Do not exit **vi**.	**:w** *filename*	113
Append contents of the editing buffer to the end of specified file. Do not exit **vi**.	**:w** >> *filename*	113
Exit **vi** without saving the contents of the editing buffer.	**:q!**	114

continued on following page

Table 4.3. (cont.) Commands used to save the editing buffer
and exit the **vi** utility

Command Function	Command Form	Page
Start editing a new file. Check to see if current editing buffer saved.	:e *filename*	116
Start editing a new file. Do not check to see if current editing buffer saved.	:e! *filename*	116
Run a shell command.	:! *shell command*	116
Start a new shell.	:!sh	--

Table 4.4. Scroll commands in the **vi** utility

Command Function	Command Form	Page
Scroll one-half screen forward.	Press control-d	117
Scroll full screen forward.	Press control-f	117
Scroll one-half screen backward.	Press control-u	117
Scroll full screen backward.	Press control-b	117

Table 4.5. Commands that cause cursor movement in the **vi** utility.

Command Function	Command Form	Page
Move cursor forward by the space.	*number* l or *number* press space bar	118
Move cursor backward by the space.	*number* h or *number* press backspace key	118
Move cursor forward by the word. Punctuation marks count as a word.	*number* w	119

continued on following page

Table 4.5. (cont.) Commands that cause cursor movement
in the **vi** utility.

Command Function	Command Form	Page
Move cursor forward by the word. Punctuation marks do not count as a word.	*number* **W**	119
Move cursor backward by the word. Punctuation marks count as a word.	*number* **b**	120
Move cursor backward by the word. Punctuation marks do not count as a word.	*number* **B**	120
Move cursor forward to the end of word. Punctuation marks count as a word.	*number* **e**	120
Move cursor forward to the end of word. Punctuation marks do not count as a word.	*number* **E**	120
Move cursor to a specific column.	*number* |	119
Move cursor forward by the line to the beginning of the line.	*number* + or *number* Return	120
Move cursor forward by the line. Maintain same column position.	*number* **j** or *number* control-n	120
Move cursor backward by the line to the beginning of the line.	*number* -	120
Move cursor backward by the line. Maintain same column position.	*number* **k** or *number* control-p	120
Move cursor forward by the sentence.	*number*)	--
Move cursor backward by the sentence.	*number* (	---
Move cursor forward by the paragraph.	*number* {	--
Move cursor backward by the paragraph.	*number* }	--
Move cursor to the end of the current line.	$	119

Table 4.6. Text insertion commands for the **vi** utility

Command Function	Command Form	Page
Insert text before the cursor.	i	121
Insert text before the first character of the current line.	I	122
Insert text after the cursor.	a	122
Insert text after the last character of the current line.	A	123
Insert text at the beginning of a new line below the current line.	o	123
Insert text at the beginning of a new line above the current line.	O	124

Table 4.7. Text deletion commands for the **vi** utility

Command Function	Command Form	Page
Deleting characters forward.	*number* **x**	125
Deleting character backward.	*number* **X**	126
Deleting words.	*number* **dw** or *number* **Dw**	127
Deleting words from the beginning of a line.	**d0**	128
Deleting from the end of a line.	**d$**	128
Deleting entire lines.	*number* **dd**	129

Table 4.8.   Text substitution commands for the vi utility

Command Function	Command Form	Page
Replace a single character.	r + *character*	130
Replacing more than one character.	R	131
Changing words.	*number* cw or *number* Cw	131
Changing lines.	*number* cc	132
Undoing the last change made in the editing buffer.	u	134
Repeating the last change made in the editing buffer.	.	135

Table 4.9.   Search commands for the vi utility.

Command Function	Command Form	Page
Searching forward in the file.	/search string	135
Searching backward in the file.	?search string	135
Repeating the previous search.	n	135
Searching in the opposite direction for the previous search string.	N	136

5
File and Information Management

In chapter 3 we gained a general understanding of the UNIX file system. In chapter 4 we learned how to use the **ex**, **ed** and **vi** editors to create text files. In this chapter we will discuss a number of UNIX utilities that enable UNIX users to manipulate the information stored in files.

Sorting a File

The **sort** utility is used to sort and merge files. This utility can sort according to several different methods. **sort** has the following form:

sort *filenames*

143

where *filenames* represents a list of one or more files. The **sort** command orders the file by the value of the ASCII codes of the characters at the beginning of each line. If more than one file is present, the files are merged into one ordered list. The results of the **sort** command are displayed on the screen.

sort OPTIONS

The following options are available to modify the method used to accomplish the sort:

b Causes leading blanks in the comparison field to be ignored.

d Causes only letters, digits, and blanks to be significant in the sort. This is called "dictionary order."

f Causes the case to be ignored. That is, all uppercase letters are treated as their lowercase counterparts.

n Causes a numerical sort. This option is intended for use with numerical data.

r Causes a reverse sort. That is, from "z" to "a" or from highest to lowest.

The **sort** command with options specified has the following form:

sort *-options filenames*

where *options* represents a list of one or more of the options listed above.

For example, the following command:

sort -fr Inventory

would cause the file **inventory** to be sorted in reverse alphabetical order with case ignored.

SPECIFYING A DIFFERENT SORT KEY

The **sort** utility normally uses the first entry on a line as the sort key. **sort** can also be used to sort on information contained in the middle or at the end of the file. For example suppose we were sorting a mailing list.

```
Mitchell Michael L 121 West Green Street Clarkston IA 53712
Ishimoto Shinako 30700 Lakeshore Blvd. Grove PA 27894
Platko Joe G 26870 Forest Drive Pontiac MI 33578
Mooney Karen K 532 Harmony Lane Severn MD 24214
Mooney Karen K 137 East Drive Severn MD 24214
```

Since we already know how to sort this file based on the first character in each line, we can sort it by last name. Suppose however that we wanted to sort by the zip code. To do so we must use a special form of the **sort** utility. Before discussing this special form, we must first understand how UNIX defines individual fields in a line of text.

A **field** can be defined as a string of non-blank characters separated by a blank space. Therefore the following fields would be defined for our first and second mailing list entries:

```
Mitchell Michael L 121 West Green Street Clarkston   IA 53712
   1       2    3  4    5    6    7       8        9  10

Ishimoto Shinako 30700 Lakeshore Blvd  Grove       PA 27894
   1       2       3       4      5      6         7   8
```

Notice that in our first entry, the zip code is indicated as field 10 while in the second it is field 8. This discrepancy is due to Mr. Ishimoto's not having a middle initial and Mr. Mitchell's street name consisting of three words compared to two for Mr. Ishimoto's street name.

Obviously to sort the file we'll have to define and organize the individual fields so they occupy the same relative position within the text line. This is accomplished by choosing a **field delimiter**. The colon (:) is often used for this purpose.

We might reorganize our file as follows using field delimiters.

```
Mitchell:Michael:L:121 West Green Street:Clarkston:IA:53712
Ishimoto:Shinako::30700 Lakeshore Blvd:Grove:PA:27894
Platko:Joe:G:26876 Forest Drive:Pontiac:MI:33578
Mooney:Karen:K:532 Harmony Lane: Severn:MD:24213
Mooney:Karen:K:137 East Drive:Severn:MD:24214
```

Notice how we allocate for an empty middle name field in Mr. Ishimoto's file by including two consecutive colons. Also notice that we did not begin or end any of the fields with a blank space. Since **sort** regards a blank space as a character, if a blank character was inadvertently included at the beginning of a field the sort would be inaccurate (unless of course the b option was indicated).

Suppose we wanted to sort our mailing list using the zip code field as the key. We could do so with the following command:

sort -t: +6 mailing

Notice that we have used a new option **-t**. This option indicates that the character following it (in this case the colon) is being used as the field delimiter. +6 tells **sort** to skip 6 fields to find the sort key. The results of executing this command would be as follows:

```
Mooney:Karen:K:137 East Drive:Severn:MD:24214
Mooney:Karen:K:532 Harmony Lane:Severn:MD:24214
Ishimoto:Shinako::30700 Lakeshore Blvd:Grove:PA:27894
Platko:Joe:G:26876 Forest Drive:Pontiac:MI:33578
Mitchell:Michael:L:121 West Green Street:Clarkston:IA:53712
```

Notice that lines 1 and 2 had identical zip codes, last names, first names, and middle initials. Upon encountering identical fields, **sort** continues its comparison with the remaining fields in the line. You can indicate at which field **sort** should stop the comparison by adding that field number preceded by a minus sign to the command line. For example,

sort -t: +1 -3 mailing

would cause the sort to occur on the second and third fields.

You can include additional **sort** parameters to specify a search based on multiple fields. For instance,

sort -t: +6 -7 +3 mailing

would specify a primary sort based on the seventh field. Additional sorting will begin with field 4 to the end of the line.

SORTING ON A SINGLE CHARACTER

You can use the form of **sort** discussed in the last section to sort on a specific character within a field. To do so add a decimal point to the number of fields to be skipped and specify the number of characters within that field to be skipped. For example,

sort +6.3 mailing

would begin the sort on the second to last digit of the zip code in our mailing list example.

The **sort** options discussed earlier can be specified for all of the fields or for just one field. If the option is added to the end of a field parameter, then the global option will be cancelled for that field. For example,

sort -r +0 -1 +6r mailing

would result in a reverse sort on the first field and a numerical sort on field 7.

Copying Files

UNIX includes a number of commands that can be used in comparing files. We'll discuss four of these; **cmp, comm, diff,** and **uniq**.

cmp

cmp compares two files and returns the positions where they differ. An execution of **cmp** might result in a screen display such as the following:

```
$cmp texta textb
texta textb differ: char 2 line 5
$
```

comm

The **comm** utility is used to find lines common to two files or unique in one of the files. The two files should be arranged in ASCII sequence before the comparison is made. This arrangement can be accomplished using the **sort** utility with no options or parameters except the files to be sorted.

The **comm** utility produces three columns of output. The first column contains the lines unique to the first file. The second column contains the lines unique to the second file. The third column contains lines common to both files.

The **comm** utility includes three options; 1, 2, and 3. The 1 option suppresses printing of the first column. The 2 and 3 options perform an identical function for the second and third columns. The **comm** command has the following form:

comm *-options first second*

where *first* and *second* represent the names of the files to be compared.

For example, the following command:

comm -12 inventory.march inventory.april

would cause the lines common to both **inventory.march** and **inventory.april** to be displayed on the screen. Note that it makes no sense to specify all three of the options.

diff

diff is used to compare two files and display the differences between them. These differences are displayed in the form of instructions that can be used to edit the files so they are identical. **diff** is used with the following configuration:

diff [options] *filename1 filename2*

diff always displays editing instructions which presume that *filename1* is to be converted to *filename2*. Keeping this in mind, let's examine some examples of **diff**.

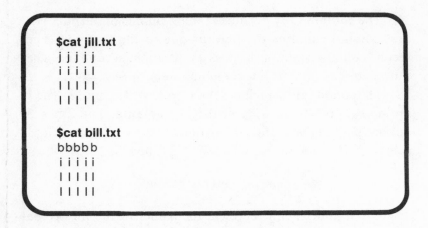

```
$cat jill.txt
j j j j j
i i i i l
l l l l l
l l l l l

$cat bill.txt
b b b b b
i i i i i
l l l l l
l l l l l
```

```
$diff jill.txt bill.txt
1c1
< j j j j j
---
> bbbbb
$
```

The first line output (*1c1*) indicates the change to be made using the following format:

Three actions can be indicated: **a** for add, **c** for change, **d** for delete.

The remainder of the **diff** display identifies those lines in *filename1* and *filename2* which are to be changed. The less-than symbol (<) prefixes lines from *filename1* while the greater-than (>) symbol prefixes lines from *filename2*.

In our example, **diff** indicates that line 1 in **jill.txt** (jjjjj) must be changed so that it matches line 1 from **bill.txt** (bbbbb).

Let's examine some more **diff** examples.

```
$cat jil.txt
 j j j j j
 i i i i i
 l l l l l

$cat jill.txt
 j j j j j
 i i i i i
 l l l l l
 l l l l l
```

```
$diff jil.txt jill.txt
 3 a 4
>l l l l l
 $
```

In the preceding example **diff** indicates that you must append line 4 from *filename2* after line 3 of *filename1*.

Let's reverse **jil.txt** and **jill.txt** for an example of a line indicated for deletion.

```
$diff jill.txt jil.txt
4 d 3
< I I I I I
$
```

Here **diff** indicates that the fourth line must be deleted from *filename1* in order for it to match *filename2*.

Generally a number of lines will be indicated by **diff** as shown in the following example.

```
$cat jello
j j j j j
e e e e e
I I I I I
I I I I I
o o o o o
$diff jil jello
2 c 2
< i i i i i
---
> e e e e e
3a 4,5
> I I I I I
> o o o o o
$
```

When two lines are separated by a comma, that range of lines is indicated.

bdiff — COMPARING LARGE FILES

The **bdiff** utility is used to compare files too large for the **diff** command. The **bdiff** command uses the same format as **diff**. **bdiff** splits the file into smaller segments and invokes **diff** on each segment.

diff3 — COMPARING THREE FILES

The **diff3** utility allows three files to be compared. The **diff3** command will display the differing ranges in the text. The following indicators are used:

> = = = = All three files are different.
>
> = = = **1** First file is different.
>
> = = = **2** Second file is different.
>
> = = = **3** Third file is different.

The **diff3** command has the following form:

> **diff3** *first second third*

where *first*, *second*, and *third* represent the names of the files to be compared.

uniq — ELIMINATING DUPLICATE TEXT LINES

UNIX's **uniq** command reads a file that has been created by sorting and merging two other files, compares the merged file's adjoining lines, eliminates duplicate lines, and outputs the remaining lines to a terminal or to a file. **uniq** is used with the following format:

> **uniq** [*options*] *filename1* [*filename2*]

filename1 indicates the file whose lines are to be compared. *filename2* is an optional parameter which specifies the file to which **uniq**'s output is to be sorted. The available options are:

-**u** results in only those lines being output which are not duplicated. In other words, any duplicated lines will be eliminated entirely.

-**d** outputs one copy of just the duplicate lines.

-**c** results in normal output except that each line is prefixed with the number of times it appears in the file.

Searching Files

UNIX includes several commands for searching files. We will discuss three of these: **grep, find, awk**.

grep

The **grep** utility is used to search a file for the occurrence of a particular string of characters. The **grep** command has the following form:

grep -*options search string filenames*

where *options* represents a line of one or more of the options detailed below, *search string* represents the string being sought, and *filenames* represents a list of one or more files to be searched. Some of the **grep** command's more useful options include:

v	Display all lines except those that match.
c	Display only the total number of matches.
n	Each line that matches is displayed with its line number in the file.

y   Causes case to be not significant in the search.

f *filename*   Causes the search string to be taken from the specified file instead of from the command line.

For example, the following command:

grep oil inventory

would cause every line that contains "oil" to be displayed on the screen. Note that a simple search pattern with only a few letters specified in the search string can result in more information than was really desired being accessed. In the previous example, entries such as coil and soil would also be found. A less ambiguous example follows:

grep 'motor oil' inventory

This command would be more likely to access only the intended entry in the file. Note the use of quote marks to set off the search string. It is necessary to set off the search string if it contains internal blanks.

find

UNIX's **find** utility allows you to search a directory and its subdirectories for files that meet a specified criteria. Once **find** has located these files, you can display their filenames, remove them, or perform a number of other operations.

The best means of illustrating **find**'s usage is to begin with an example. The following commands:

$find . -name '*.txt'

would find all files in the current working directory and its subdirectories (.) for those files with filenames (**-name**) that have an extension of .txt. Note that we enclosed our filename in single quotes in this example, this is only required if a filename match character is included.

Our preceding example is useful in that it illustrates how **find** is used, however since **find** does not do anything with these files once they are located, our example serves no other purpose. Let's modify our example as follows so that **find** not only locates the indicated files but also displays these:

$find . -name '*.txt' -print

As you may already have surmised, three parameters may be indicated with **find**: a *directory*, a *search criteria*, and an *action criteria*. **find**'s general configuration follows:

find *directory searchcriteria parameter actioncriteria parameter*

find's search criteria are listed in table 5.1 while its action criteria appear in table 5.2.

Table 5.1. **find** search criteria

Search Criteria	Parameter	Description
-name	*filename*	Files whose names match *filename* will meet this search criteria. If *filename* includes a match character (*, ?) it must be enclosed within single quotes.
-type	*filetype* b block special c character special file d directory file f plain file	Files whose type matches that specified will meet the search criteria.
-links	$\pm x$	Files with the number of links indicated by $\pm$ x meet this criteria.

continued on following page

Table 5.1. (cont.)   **find** search criteria

Search Criteria	Parameter	Description
-user	*login name* or *user ID number*	Files belonging to the user with the indicated *login name* or *user ID number* meet this criteria.
-group	*group name* or *group ID number*	Files belonging to the group with the indicated *group name* or *group ID number* meet this criteria.
-size	$\pm x$	Files greater than the size indicated by +x in bytes or less than the size indicated by -x in bytes will meet this criteria.
-atime	$\pm x$	Files not accessed within the number of days specified by +x will meet this criteria. Files accessed within the number of days specified by -x will meet this criteria. If $\pm$ is not indicated, files accessed x days ago will be returned.
-mtime	$\pm x$	Files not modified within the number of days specified by +x will meet this criteria. Files modified within the number of days specified by -x will meet this criteria. If $\pm$ is not indicated, files modified x days ago will be returned.
-newer	*filename*	Files modified more recently than *filename* will meet this criteria.

Table 5.2. **find** action criteria

Search Criteria	Parameter	Description
-print		**find** displays the pathname of the file it is evaluating if the search criteria are met.
-exec	*command* { } \;	**exec** executes the indicated *command* if the preceding search criteria are met. The pair of braces indicate the filename, and \; is used to end the command.
-ok	*command* { } \;	**ok** functions exactly like **exec** except that the user is prompted before the *command* is executed. A "y" must be input for the command to execute.

find can be implemented for a variety of different purposes as the following examples illustrate:

find /usr -size -100 -exec rm { } **\;**
find . /user/sam -name 'memo.*' -print
find /usr/bill -name '*.txt' -ok rm {} **\;**

In the first example, **find** locates all files in the **usr** directory and its subdirectories with a size less than 100 bytes and removes these. In the second example, find locates all files whose names match 'memo.*' in the working directory and in Sam's home directory and displays these. Note that two directories can be specified. In the third example any files in Bill's home directory with the extension .txt will be removed if the user responds with a 'y' to the ok prompt.

Finally the following three operators can be used with the search criteria:

!

blank space

-o

If a ! precedes a search, the criteria is reversed. If our third example was modified as follows:

find /usr/bill ! -name '*.txt' -ok rm { } \;

only those files in Bill's home directory whose names did not end in .txt would be prompted for removal.

If two or more search criteria are separated by blank spaces in a **find** command, a file must meet all criteria. If our third example was modified as follows:

find /usr/bill -name '*.txt' -newer filea -ok rm { } \;

only those files in Bill's working directory with extensions of .txt that had been revised more recently than **filea** would be prompted for removal.

An **-o** indicates that if either of the search criteria are satisfied the file will be returned. For example,

find /usr/bill -name -o '*.txt' -newer filea -ok rm { } \;

would result in those files in Bill's working directory that had extensions of .txt or that had been revised more recently than **filea** being prompted for removal.

awk

awk is one of UNIX's most powerful utilities. **awk** can be used to search one or more files to determine which if any lines match a specific pattern. Once **awk** finds such a line, it processes that line according to instructions included with the command.

For example, **awk** could search an inventory file similar to that listed below,

Description	Quantity	Cost per unit
widgets	19	.50
gadgets	21	.32
whatsits	10	1.75

for a particular item (let's say gadgets), use information in that item's text line (quantity and price) and generate additional information (such as the value of the gadget stock). In this respect, **awk** is a programming language in itself and can function in a manner much like a spreadsheet program.

awk is used with either of the following two configurations:

> **awk** *program filenames*
> **awk -f** *programfilenames filenames*

In the first configuration, the program that **awk** is to execute is specified in the command line. In the second configuration, the program is stored as the file given in *programfilename*. The -f option instructs **awk** to read this file.

awk executes the program specified in *program* or *programfilename* on the file or files denoted by *filenames*. An **awk** program consists of two parts: a pattern and an action. The action must be enclosed in braces to differentiate it from the pattern as shown in the simple **awk** program given below:

> /twisted/ {print}

This program would search the indicated files for lines which contained the word twisted. (Note that string patterns are enclosed within slashes). These lines would then be routed to the standard output device by the print action.

awk programs can include both user and program variables, operators, functions, and other features such as BEGIN, END, output(>), append(>>), piping (|), and comments (#). We'll discuss these features using example programs.

awk allows both program variables and user variables in either the pattern or action portion of the program. The program variables are as follows:

NR	current record number
$0	the current record
$l-$x	the fields in the current record
NF	the number of fields in the current record
FS	input field separator ([SPACE] or [TAB])
OFS	output field separator ([SPACE])
RS	input record separator (new line character)
ORS	output record separator (new line character)
FILENAME	current input filename (new line character)

The default values for the input and output record and field separators are listed above. These values can be altered by assigning a new value to its associated variable.

The following program will output the second field of all lines containing the pattern widgets:

```
/widgets/ {print $2}
```

An **awk** program can also include user-defined variables.

```
/widgets/ {sum1+=$2}
END {print "The total no. of widgets is" sum1}
```

This program accumulates the contents of field 2 for those lines containing the pattern string widgets in the user variable sum1. Notice the use of END in this program. **awk** executes actions specified after END after all of the specified files have been processed. In our example, after **awk** has searched the indicated files and accumulated a figure in sum1, the string constant and user variable included with print will be output.

BEGIN can be used in a similar fashion to cause **awk** to execute an action prior to processing the specified files.

Our preceding example also illustrates the fact that the following arithmetic operators can be used in an **awk** program:

+=	++	*=
*	--	/=
/	+=	%=
%	-=	

An **awk** program can also include the following relational operators:

<	!=
<=	>=
==	>

as well as the Boolean operators ‖ (Or) and && (And).

awk also includes the following special operators:

~

!~

The tilde (~) operator tests for equality between a field and/or a variable and a pattern. ~! tests for inequality between a field and/or variable and a pattern. For example, the following **awk** program,

```
$3~/[a-z]/ {print NR $3}
```

would output the record number and field 3 of those lines whose third field contained only a single lower-case alpha character.

awk programs can include the following functions:

length   returns the number of characters in the specified argument. If an argument is not included, length returns the number of characters in the current input record.

substr(string,x,y)	returns a substring from string that begins at the xth character in string and is y characters in length.
int	returns the integer portion of its argument.

The following **awk** program uses the length function to eliminate all lines with less than 100 characters:

length>100 {print}

The redirection and piping operators can also be used in an **awk** program. > can be used to direct print's output to the specified file; >> will append that output to a file; and | will pipe the output as input to another program. We can modify our previous **awk** program as follows to send the output to **fileb**:

length>100 {print>**fileb**}

Finally, **awk** can be specified with two patterns delimited with a comma. In such cases, **awk** will match a range of lines from the specified file. The beginning line of the range will be the first line that matches the first pattern. The last line of the range will be the next line that matches the record pattern. For example the following **awk** program,

$1>0,$1<0 {print}

would select as the first line of its range the first line from the specified file with a value in field 1 greater than 0. That line as well as all subsequent lines would be output until a line was encountered with a value in field 1 less than 0.

Splitting a File

Splitting a large file into two or more smaller files makes the file much easier to manage. The split should usually be made at the logical breaks in the file. For instance, in an alphabetical inventory file, a logical place to split the file would be between words beginning with "m" and "n".

bfs — SCANNING A LARGE FILE

Before splitting a file, it is a good idea to scan it. A file too large to be handled by a text editor can be scanned manually. A scan is generally performed to determine where a file should be broken when it is to be split into smaller files. The **bfs** utility is used to accomplish such a task. The **bfs** command has the following form:

bfs *filename*

where filename is the name of the file to be scanned. Once the **bfs** command has been issued, the specified file can be viewed using **ed** address commands such as +, -, and line numbers.

For example, the following command:

bfs etc/termcap

would cause /**etc**/**termcap** to be specified. A command such as **1,20p** would cause the first twenty lines of the /**etc**/**termcap** file to be displayed on the screen.

The **q** command is used to exit the **bfs** utility. Simply type **q** and press the Return key.

split — SIMPLE SPLIT

The **split** utility is used to divide a large file into several, arbitrarily sized, smaller files. Each of the new files will be the same size except for the last file. The last file may vary depending on the portion of the original file remaining to be stored in it. The split command has the following form:

split *-size original resulting*

where *size* represents the number of lines that the resulting files will contain, *original* represents the name of the original file, and *resulting* represents a name assigned to the newly created files containing the split. Note that each of these files will have a suffix appended to it. The first will have an **aa**, the second an **ab**, etc.

For example, the following command:

split -100 /etc/termcap splitcap

might cause the **/etc/termcap** file to be split into five files: **splitcapaa, splitcapab, splitcapac, splitcapad**, and **splitcapae**. Assuming **termcap** to be 440 lines in length, each of these files would be 100 lines long except for **splitcapae** which would contain 40 lines. Note that the file is divided without regard to the file contents. The user has little control over where the breaks occur. Also, the **split** utility does not alter the original file.

csplit — CONTROLLED SPLIT

The **csplit** utility allows the user to split a file so that the breaks occur in selected spots. The **csplit** utility allows a large file to be split at logical breaks in the file's text. The **csplit** command has the following form:

csplit -f *resulting   original   line numbers*

where *original* represents the name of the file to be split, *line numbers* represents a list of one or more line numbers within the file *original* at which the splits will be made, and *resulting* represents the name of the resulting file. Note that each file will have a two digit suffix. The first will be **00,** the second **01**, and so forth.

For example, suppose we had a very long file named **inventory**, that contained our store inventory in alphabetical order. We could split this long file into smaller, more manageable files. The file must first be scanned using the **bfs** utility. The line numbers of those lines that are to be the first line in one of the smaller files should be noted. For the purposes of the example, we will split the file into three smaller files. Suppose the first entry in the **inventory** file beginning with the letter "h" occurs at line 2192. Similarly, the first occurrence of the letter "p" occurs at line 4519. The following command:

csplit -f inventory, inventory 2192 4519

would cause the **inventory** file to be split into three smaller files. The name and contents of each resulting file follows:

inventory.00   All entries from the **inventory** file beginning with the letters "a" through "g".

inventory.01   All entries from the **inventory** file beginning with the letters "h" through "o".

inventory.02   All entries from the **inventory** file beginning with the letters "p" through "z".

Note that the **csplit** command does not alter the contents of the original file.

Obtaining Statistics On File Size

The **wc** utility is used to gather statistics regarding the size of files. The **wc** utility reports the file size in units of lines, words, and characters. The **wc** command has the following form:

wc [-*lwc*] *filenames*

filenames represents a list of one or more files that are to be reported upon. -*l* results in only the number of lines being displayed; -*w* displays the number of words; and -*c* displays the number of characters.

For example, the following command:

wc   inventory.00   inventory.01   inventory.02

would cause a display similar to the following:

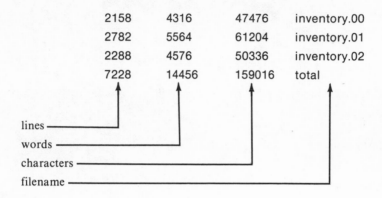

2158	4316	47476	inventory.00
2782	5564	61204	inventory.01
2288	4576	50336	inventory.02
7228	14456	159016	total

lines

words

characters

filename

6

The Shell

The shell is the interface between the UNIX kernel and the system user. The shell is essentially a command interpreter. That is, it executes the commands entered by the system user. For example, if the **who** command was entered, the shell would locate and execute this utility.

The shell can also be used as a programming language. Commands can be combined to accomplish specific tasks. Once developed, a combination of commands can be stored as a file and later invoked like any other utility. UNIX features such as piping, redirection, shell scripts, shell variables and metacharacters can be used in shell programming to develop sophisticated applications.

169

In this chapter we'll begin our discussion of the shell by examining the command line and redirection of its input and output. We'll then discuss shell programming.

THE SHELL AS A COMMAND INTERPRETER

The Command Line

Although we've already had some experience with the command line, an examination of it in more detail is in order. The configuration for the command line is as follows:

command [*option*][*argument*]

In the following example of a command line entry,

sort -r customer.txt

sort is the command name, **-r** is an option available for use with **sort** and **customer.txt** is the argument, which in this case is the same as the name of the file to be sorted.

Blank spaces are used to separate entries on the command line. Therefore, if you entered,

sort-r customer.txt

UNIX would search for a command named **sort-r**.

Notice in our preceding example that the option (**-r**) was prefixed with a hyphen. This is typical with UNIX command options. In some instances, you may wish to specify two or more options with a command. These multiple options can be entered using two different methods. First, spaces can be used to delimit each option as in the following command line:

sort -b -r -u customer.txt

The multiple options can also be specified as a single group as long as the group is prefixed with a single hyphen as shown in the following command line example:

sort -bru customer.txt

Either of the following command line entries would be incorrect:

sort -b-r-u customer.txt
sort -b r u customer.txt

We already included commands which have more than 1 argument. In such instances, each of the arguments must be separated by a blank space as shown below:

rm memo.to.sam memo.to.bill

If you wish to include more than one command on a command line, you can do so by separating them with a semicolon.

The backslash can be used to extend a command over more than one line. The shell will display the > prompt rather than the $ prompt on subsequent lines to notify the user that the command entry has not been completed.

Redirection

We've already briefly touched on several of UNIX's redirection operators. As you may recall, these enable a UNIX user to redirect the output from or input to a UNIX command. Generally, a UNIX command takes its input from the terminal keyboard and displays its output on the terminal screen. Redirection operators allow the input to a command to be taken from a different source, such as a file. The output from a command can also be sent to a different source, such as a file or another UNIX command.

REDIRECTING INPUT

The less than symbol (<) is used to indicate redirection of input. This redirection technique has the following form:

command < filename

where *command* represents a UNIX command that usually receives input from the keyboard, and *filename* represents the name of a file that contains the input for the command.

For example, the following command:

mail helen tom < memo

would cause the file **memo** to be mailed to both **helen** and **tom**.

REDIRECTING OUTPUT

Output that is redirected to a file can either be appended to the end of the file or used to overwrite the current contents of the file. The file will be created if it did not previously exist.

The greater than symbol (>) is used to indicate redirection of output that will overwrite the existing file. This redirection technique has the following form:

command > filename

where *command* represents a UNIX command that usually produces output for display on the terminal's screen, and *filename* represents the name of the file to be overwritten by the command's output.

The > redirection operator is particularly useful for combining two or more files. For example, the following command:

cat address body > letter

would cause the files **address** and **body** to be written in the file **letter**. The file **address** would appear first.

APPENDING

The greater than symbol (>) is used twice in succession to indicate redirection of output that will be appended to an existing file. This redirection technique has the following form:

command >> filename

where *command* represents a UNIX command that usually produces output for display on the screen, and *filename* represents the name of the file to be added to by the command's output:

For example, the following command:

cat postscript >> letter

would cause the file **postscript** to be appended to the end of the file **letter**.

COMBINING REDIRECTION OPERATORS

The redirection operators can be combined as shown in the following example:

$ed texta < corrections > textb

Here **texta** would receive its input from **corrections** with the output being redirected to **textb**.

The redirection operators can also be combined in the following order:

$ed texta > corrections < textb

Here the output from **textb** is directed to the file **corrections** which is used as input for the file **textb**.

Note that two or more inputs (or outputs) cannot be combined on the same command line. For example,

$ed texta > corrections > textb

would be illegal.

PIPES

One limitation of the redirection operators is that they cannot be used to redirect input or output from one command to another. They can only be used to redirect input to a command from a file or output from a command to a file. The redirection operators can be used with intermediate steps to indirectly link a command to a command as shown below:

```
$who > tempfile
$lpr tempfile
$rm tempfile
```

The first command redirects the names of the system users to a temporary file, **tempfile**. In the second command line, **lpr** prints **tempfile** which is then removed in the third command line.

Obviously we could eliminate the extra steps in the preceding example if an operator was available that designated the output of the command as the input for another. UNIX's pipeline operator allows us to do exactly that as shown below:

$who|lpr

Pipes can be used to quickly build a facility to accomplish a specific task. The utilities are used as the basic building blocks, and pipes are used to transfer the information between the utilities. Such a structure is often called a pipeline.

The vertical bar (|) is used to represent a pipeline. The pipe symbol is placed after the utility that places information into it but before the utility that takes information from the pipe. A pipe between two utilities has the following form:

producer | consumer

where *producer* represents the command that inputs data and *consumer* represents the command that receives data.

For example, a simple use of a pipe follows:

who | wc -l

This sequence of commands would cause a display similar to the following:

```
$who | wc -l
2

$
```

Since the **who** command displays the users currently logged onto the computer, one to a line, and the **wc -l** command counts the lines, the output tells us that two users are currently logged onto the system.

We will now give a more complicated example. The following sequence:

sort inventory I uniq I wc -I > result

would cause the number of unique lines in the **inventory** file to be stored in the file **result**.

FILTERS

A **filter** is a UNIX utility that was designed to receive its input from the standard input device (the terminal), process that input and send the output to the standard output device (the display). **sort** and **uc** are examples of filters.

UNIX's redirection operators and pipeline can be used to send the output from a filter to a file or to another command. For example, the following command:

$who I wc -I I lpr

would in effect cause the number of system users to be output on the printer. Notice how diverse UNIX utilities can be combined to achieve the result you desire.

INPUT/OUTPUT DEVICES

Redirection is possible in UNIX because input and output devices such as the printer or terminal are all regarded as files. Each device is assigned a filename which is stored in the **/dev** directory. For example your terminal's device name might be **/dev/tty02**. You can display your terminal's pathname by entering the **tty** command.

Most UNIX commands use the terminal by default as their input and output file. For example,

$who

could be interpreted as:

$who /dev/tty02

Therefore when we use a redirection operator, we are actually just indicating a filename other than the default.

THE SHELL AS A PROGRAMMING LANGUAGE

We've already seen how the shell executes commands entered by the user. In this respect the shell is used as a command interpreter.

UNIX's shell can be used as a programming language as well as a command interpreter. When the shell is used as a programming language, it executes a series of commands which had been previously stored in a file known as a **shellscript**.

In the following sections, we'll examine how the shell can be used as a programming language. We'll examine how to create and execute a shellscript, and we'll discuss a number of options that can be used in shell programming such as arguments, shell variables, processes, and program control commands.

Creating a Shellscript

A shellscript can be created like any other UNIX file using one of the editors. Suppose we created a shellscript named **pgma** that contained the command **$who am i**. If you try to execute **pgma**, an error message will appear as shown on the following page:

```
$pgma
pgma: cannot execute
$
```

The reason that **pgma** would not execute is that the shell does not regard it as an executable file.

Before **pgma** can be executed, it must be designated as an executable file. UNIX's **chmod** utility allows you to accomplish this task by changing the file's access privileges. Suppose we used the **ls -l** command to display **pgma**'s access permissions.

```
$ls -l pgma
-rw-rw-r-- 2 jetrink 24 May 10 9:51 pgma
```

Note that **pgma**'s owner has read and write permission but not execute permission. We can execute **chmod** as shown below to give the owner execute access privileges to **pgma**.

```
$chmod u+x pgma
$ls -l pgma
-rwxrw-r-- 2 jetrink 24 May 9:52 pgma
  ↑
  execute access privilege
```

chmod's argument (**u+x**) can be interpreted as adding (+) execute access (**x**) for the owner (**u**) for the file (**pgma**). Note in the preceding screen display the x indicates that the owner now has execute access privileges.

As shown in the following screen display, the shellscript can now be executed as a command:

```
$pgma
jetrink      tty2      may 24 9:53
$
```

Command Line Argument Variables

When a shellscript is executed with arguments, the shell stores the first nine arguments in the variables $1, $2,...$9. $* indicates all of the arguments ; $0 denotes the shell script itself; and $# returns the number of arguments on the command line.

Usage of variables to denote command line arguments is illustrated in the following example:

```
$cat display
echo ' The command line arguments'
echo 'are' $1 $2 $3 $4 $5
$display one two three four five
The command line arguments
are one two three four five
```

Variables & Shell Programming

The shell uses string variables to keep track of information. These variables can be categorized as:

- user variables
- shell variables

User variables are defined by the system user. Shell variables are a set of standard, built-in variables that keep track of important system information such as the search path, home directory, shell prompt, mail path, etc.

USER VARIABLES

User variables are defined as follows:

$ leader=alice

The preceding line initializes the variable leader and assigns it the value alice. Spaces are not allowed on either side of the equals sign. To indicate a variable's value in a command line, the variable must be preceded with a $.

```
$echo leader
leader
$echo $leader
alice
$
```

Note that the variable name is treated as a literal if it is not prefixed with a $.

A user variable can be defined as read-only (that is it cannot be changed) using UNIX's **readonly** command. Remember to assign the variable's value prior to executing **readonly**.

```
$leader=alice
$readonly leader
$leader=jane
  leader: is readonly
$readonly
  readonly leader
$
```

Note that when **readonly** is executed without an argument, it displays the current readonly variables.

---

* **echo** copies its arguments to the standard output.

SHELL VARIABLES

As we mentioned earlier, the shell must have access to certain pieces of information such as the user's home directory, the mail directory, the prompt, and information pertaining to the terminal. The shell stores this information in certain predefined shell variables. You can display the current shell variables by executing the **set** command.

```
$set
HOME=/usr/bill
IFS=

MAIL=/usr/mail/bill
PATH=.:/bin:/usr/bin
PS1=$
PS2=>
TERM=
$
```

HOME is used to store the pathname of the user's home directory.

IFS (internal field separator) contains a list of the characters that can be used to delimit words on a command line. These are normally the blank space, the tab, and the newline character (which is generated when the return key is pressed). Since the command line delimiter characters are generally specified as invisible characters, in most instances nothing will appear after IFS. Note, however, that the inclusion of the newline character in IFS causes an extra blank line to appear in the output.

MAIL contains the directory where the user's mail is sent.

PATH stores the directories where the shell will search for commands. A colon is used to delimit the various directories. PATH is defined by default as follows:

PATH = .:$HOME/bin:/bin:/usr/bin:

The preceding PATH variable directs the shell to search for a command beginning with the current directory. The search then continues with the /**bin** (sub)directory under the **$HOME** directory, the /**bin** directory, and the **bin** subdirectory in the **usr** directory.

If the user has several executable files, they should all be stored in the same place. By convention, a user's executable files are generally stored in the subdirectory of the home directory named **bin**. If this convention is followed, be sure that this subdirectory is included in the search path. The appearance of **$HOME/bin:** places the subdirectory **bin** in the search path. Note that this **bin** will be searched after the . directory but before the system's /**bin** directory. The search order is important. If the **$HOME/bin** and the /**bin** directories contain files with identical names, the first file that is found is the file that is used.

For example, suppose the user named an executable file in the **$HOME/bin** directory **who**. Then, whenever **who** was used, the search would return the file named **who** in the **$HOME/bin** directory. The file named **who** in the /**bin** directory would be ignored.

PS1 defines the shell prompt, PS2 defines the prompt used by the shell when it continues a line. TERM identifies the terminal being used.

As with user variables, we can use shell variables in a UNIX command if we prefix the variable name with the $ character.

Processes

Although UNIX includes just one shell program, there can be a number of shell processes. A *process* can be defined as a program being executed. When a user logs in, a separate shell process is created. Even though any number of shell processes might coexist at any one moment, only one shell process is actually executing. UNIX switches from running one user's shell process to the next user's, etc. Moreover, UNIX keeps each shell process separate so as to prevent one user's work from becoming confused with anothers.

PROCESS HIERARCHY

The various UNIX processes have a hierarchical structure just like the file system. The UNIX system begins operating with a root process, PID (process identification number) 1. A login process for each terminal branches from this root process. When the login is complete, the login process becomes a shell process.

When the user executes a command from the shell, the process hierarchy branches to the command process. While the command process is executing, the shell process is inactive. Once the command execution has been completed, the shell process again becomes active, and the shell prompt is displayed.

When a command is run in background (by adding a & to the end of the command line), the shell process remains active while the command process is executing. The command process's PID number is displayed while the shell process prompts for another command. In effect the command process is executed independently of the shell process.

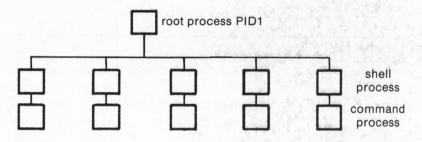

Figure 6.1. Process hierarchy

PID (Process Identification Number)

As we mentioned in the last section, each process is assigned a unique process identification number (PIN). The PIN number of the process currently being executed is stored in the $$ shell variable. The **ps** utility offers an efficient means of determining PID's. **ps** displays the status of each active process controlled by your terminal.

```
$ps
PID      TTY     TIME    CMD
13657    12-     0:04    ps
13422    12      0:08    -sh
$
```

Notice in our preceding example that two processes are executing — the shell process, which is denoted by **sh**, and **ps**. The PID column displays the process's PID number. TTY indicates the terminal. TIME displays the number of seconds that the process has been executing, and CMD indicates the command line used to activate the process.

Table 6.1. ps column descriptions

ps column	description
F (flags)	Displays the flags associated with the process.
S (state)	Displays the process's state.
UID (user ID)	Displays the user ID number of the process's owner.
PID	Displays the process ID number.
PPID	Displays the PID of the process's parents.
CPU	Usage of the central processor.
PRI	Displays the process's priority. A lower number indicates a higher priority.
NICE	A number created by the **nice** utility to calculate the process's priority.
ADDR	Process address.
SZ	Process size in blocks.
WCHAN	If the process is active, this column is empty. If the process is inactive, this column indicates the event upon which it will activate.
TTY	The terminal number that controls the process.
TIME	The number of seconds the process has been executing.
CMD	The command line used to activate the process.

ps can be executed with three options: -a, -x, and l. -a is used to display information on active processes controlled by any terminal. -x displays information on all active processes, even those not controlled by a terminal. -l results in **ps** displaying an extensive report on the actual processes as shown on the following page.

```
$ps -l
```

F	S	UID	PID	PPID	CPU	PRI	NICE	ADDR	SZ	WCHAN	TTY	TIME	CMD
1	R	103	13709	13422	78	20	20	2bc	10		12	0:04	ps -l
1	S	103	13422	1	0	30	20	3c4	9	ela5	12	0:12	-sh

The additional columns are described in table 6.1.

MULTIPLE SHELL PROCESSES

UNIX allows an individual user to create more than one shell process for himself. A new shell can be activated by executing the **sh** command. You can confirm the creation of a new shell by executing **ps** as shown below:

```
$sh
$ps
PID        TTY     TIME      COMMAND
13787      12      0:04      ps
13422      12      0:09      -sh
13690      12      0:05      -sh
```

You can continue creating new shells by executing **sh**. To close the current shell, press [CTRL-D]*.

---

* On most systems, this key logs out.

sh can execute a command as well as a new shell.

```
$cat userinfo1
$echo 'I am'
who am i
$sh userinfo1
I am
jetrink   tty 2     May 10 11:49
$
```

Note that **userinfo1** was executed under the new shell, not under the original.

Also a shellscript can be constructed so that it contains a number of commands and even other shellscripts.

```
$cat userinfo1
echo 'I am'
who am i
$cat userinfo2
usrinfo1
echo 'My directory path is'
pwd
$userinfo2
I am
jetrink      tty 2     May 10 12:01
My directory path is
/usr/jetrink/memo
$
```

---

* UNIX's **echo** command displays its arguments.

If you wish to include several commands on a single line, you can do so by delimiting each command with a semicolon.

Exporting Variables

As shown in the preceding section, one process can call another process. When one process calls another, however, the values of that's process's variables are not passed to the new process.

```
$cat menu1
dinner=veal
echo $0 $dinner
menu2
$cat menu2
echo $0 $dinner
$menu1
menu1 veal
menu2
$
```

Notice in our example that the value of dinner was not passed to the new process, **menu2**, when it was executed from **menu1**.

UNIX's **export** command allows you to pass a copy of a variable's value to the process being executed. If that copy is subsequently changed within the new process, it will not affect the value in the original process.

```
$cat menu1
export dinner
dinner=veal
echo $0 $dinner
menu2
echo 'original' $0 $dinner
$cat menu2
echo $0 $dinner
dinner=swordfish
echo 'revised' $0 $dinner
$menu1
menu1   veal
menu2   veal
revised menu2 swordfish
original menu1 veal
$
```

Notice that dinner's value is passed to **menu2** by **export**. dinner's value can be changed within **menu2** as shown in the third line output when **menu1** is executed. However, the revised value for dinner is not passed back to the original process as evidenced by the fourth line output when **menu1** is executed.

Variable values can effectively be exported when a command is executed as part of the original process. In other words a new process is not created to execute the command. UNIX's . and **exec** commands enable a command to be executed within the original process without originating a new process.

The . command executes the specified command within the original process and returns control to that process when the command's execution ends. The **exec** command does not return control to the originating process.

```
$cat menu1
dinner=veal
echo $0 $dinner
.menu2
dinner=swordfish
echo 'revised' $0 $dinner
$cat menu2
echo $0 $dinner
$menu1
menu1 veal
menu2 veal
revised menu1 swordfish
```

```
$cat menu1
dinner=veal
echo $0 $dinner
exec menu2
dinner=swordfish
echo 'revised' $0 $dinner
$cat menu2
echo 0$ $dinner
$menu1
menu1   veal
menu2   veal
$
```

Note that inclusion of the . command causes the variable's value to be passed to **menu2** as a new process was not started. When **exec** was specified, execution ended with the end of **menu2**; the third line was not output.

COMMANDS IN SHELLSCRIPTS

A command can be executed within a shellscript by enclosing it within accent characters ('). The command as well as the accent characters will be replaced by the command output.

```
$cat termpath
$term='tty'
echo 'Your terminal path is' $term
$termpath
Your terminal path is /dev/tty04
$
```

Shellscript Input and Program Control Commands

A number of commands can be used in a shellscript to allow user input and control the program's flow. We discuss a number of these in the following sections.

read

The **read** command allows the shellscript to receive input from the standard input — generally the terminal keyboard. **read**, in effect, permits the user to communicate with the shellscript.

```
$cat introduction
echo 'My name is Bourne.'
echo 'What is yours \?'
read usernam
echo 'Nice to meet you' $usernam
$introduction
My name is Bourne.
What is yours?

Steve Brodsky  ◄──── user input

Nice to meet your Steve Brodsky
$
```

Notice in our preceding example that the backslash (\ ) was used to negate the special meaning of ?, which is a match character. The **read** statement accepts one line of input and assigns it to the variable usernam.

If only one variable is specified, all data input will be assigned to that variable. If more than one variable is specified, the initial variable is assigned the first word input, the second variable is assigned to the second word input, etc. The final variable is assigned any remaining input. Excess variables are not assigned values.

for/do

The **for** command can be used to set up a loop in a shellscript. **for** is used with the following configuration:

```
for i in argument1 argument2...
  do
    command1
    command2
    .
    .
    .
  done
```

i is known as the loop index. Any variable name could be indicated for i, but by convention programmers generally use i for the loop index. **for** passes the first argument (argument1) to i and then executes the commands specified between **do** and **done**. The process then repeats with argument2 being assigned to i. When each available argument has been passed to i, program control reverts to the statement following **done**.

```
$cat car
for i in corvette transam chevette
  do
  echo 'Can I have a' i 'for graduation \?'
done
$car
  Can I have a corvette for graduation?
  Can I have a transam for graduation?
  Can I have a chevette for graduation?
$
```

for can also be used as follows:

```
for i
  do
    command 1
    command 2
    .
    .
    .
  done
```

Here i is replaced with each of the command line arguments ($1, $2, $3,...) one by one. **for** i actually implies **for** i $*.

```
$cat car
for i
   do
   echo 'Can I have a 'i' for graduation \?'
   done
$car corvette transam chevette
   Can I have a corvette for graduation?
   Can I have a transam for graduation?
   Can I have a chevette for graduation?
$
```

if/then/else

if/then statements can be used to control flow of execution of a shellscript. The configuration for **if/then** is given below:

```
if test expression
   then commands
fi
```

The **if/then** control structure sets up a condition or question. If the answer to the question evaluates as true, the commands following **then** are executed. If the answer evaluates as false, shellscript execution continues with the statement after **fi**. An example of **if/then** usage is given on the following page.

```
$cat guessit
echo 'guess my sign libra or gemini:'
read astsign
if test astsign='libra'
   then echo 'You are right'

fi
$guessit
guess my sign libra or gemini:

libra ◄————user input

You are right
$
```

else can also be included in the **if/then** command to provide an additional branching option.

```
if test expression
   then commands
   else commands
fi
```

We could modify our example as follows to include **else**:

```
$cat guessit
echo 'guess my sign libra or gemini:'
read astsign
if test astsign='libra'
   then echo 'You are right'
   else echo 'You are wrong'

fi
$guessit
guess my sign libra or gemini

gemini ◄————user input

You are wrong
$
```

case

The **case** command can also be used to branch execution within a shellscript. **case** is especially useful for defining a menu of options for the user. **case** is used with the following configuration:

```
case $choice in
   option1) command1;;
   option2) command2;;
   .
   .
   .
esac
```

The list of options is evaluated to find if any of these match $choice. If a match occurs, the command is executed. If no match occurs, execution continues with the statement following **esac**. Only one match is possible. If the options list contains more than one possible match, the match will occur on the first option. Subsequent matches will be ignored.

* can be used to match any value of $choice. Generally *) is used as the final choice is a **case** option list so that a command is indicated even if no match occurs. The following special characters are also available for use with **case**:

?	matches any one character
|	acts like the OR boolean operator. Enables a choice assuming more than one option.
[ ]	defines a character classification for a match (*see* page 61).

```
$cat menu1
echo 'choose the year'
echo 'you want to display'
echo '1=1985'
echo '2=1984'
echo '3=1983'
read $pgmnum
case $pgmnum in
    1) cal 1985 ;;
    2) cal 1984 ;;
    3) cal 1983 ;;
    *) echo 'Invalid entry'
esac
$menu1
choose the year
you want to display
1=1985
2=1984
3=1983

1 ◄────────user input
```

```
                        1985
        Jan                 Feb                 Mar
 S  M Tu  W Th  S  S    S  M Tu  W Th  F  S    S  M Tu  W Th  F  S
       1  2  3  4  5                   1  2                   1  2
 6  7  8  9 10 11 12    3  4  5  6  7  8  9    3  4  5  6  7  8  9
13 14 15 16 17 18 19   10 11 12 13 14 15 16   10 11 12 13 14 15 16
20 21 22 23 24 25 26   17 18 19 20 21 22 23   17 18 19 20 21 22 23
27 28 29 30 31         24 25 26 27 28         24 25 26 27 28 29 30
                                              31
```

(We've omitted the remaining months to conserve space.)

7

Mail

UNIX's **mail** utility allows users to communicate via messages. The **mail** services are based on the concept of physical mail. A user can send copies of a message to any number of other users, who can respond to the message if necessary.

The **mail** utility maintains a list of all messages received by each user. Until a particular message is actually disposed of by the receiving user, it remains in the system.

In this chapter, we will touch upon all facets of the **mail** facility. We will detail how to create and send messages via the **mail** system and read and dispose of incoming messages. We will also discuss special uses of the **mail** utility.

MODES

The **mail** utility has two distinct modes. These are the command mode and the compose mode. The mail utility displays a prompt (the underline character) in the compose mode.

Either mode may be invoked from the shell by the use of the **mail** command. If user names are given, the compose mode will be activated. If no user names are given, the command mode will be invoked. The compose mode may also be invoked from within the command mode. Details on all of these uses are given in the following sections.

Command Mode

The command mode is used to manipulate received messages. Received messages can be viewed, saved, or deleted. The command mode is also used to set the **mail** utility's options and for miscellaneous tasks such as running shell commands from the **mail** utility.

While in the command mode, input from the keyboard is interpreted as **mail** utility commands. We will cover the individual commands later. A help menu that displays information about these commands is available. Typing **?** and pressing the Return key from the **mail** command mode causes the screen to display the command help menu.

Compose Mode

The compose mode is used to prepare messages to be mailed. Generally, input from the keyboard is added to the message being created. Special compose mode escape commands are used to specify message headers and who should receive copies of the message. A help menu that displays information about the escape commands is available. Typing ~? and pressing the Return key from the **mail** compose mode causes the screen to display the escape command help menu.

SENDING MAIL

It is important to distinguish the parts of a message in order to best use the **mail** utility. We discuss the different parts that comprise a message before covering how to actually send a message via the **mail** system.

Anatomy of a Message

All messages sent via the **mail** utility consist of two parts, the header and the body. The header is used to specify information pertinent to the message. The body contains the main text of the message.

THE HEADER

The information contained in the header tells the **mail** utility where to deliver the message. The header also informs the recipient about the message. The header contains the following fields:

- From
- To
- Date
- Subject
- Carbon Copies (Cc)
- Blind Carbon Copies (Bcc)
- Return Receipt To

The **From** field is used to specify the sender of the message. The **mail** utility automatically sets this field to the login name of the user who sent the message.

The **To** field specifies the recipients of the message. The users who are to receive the message must be specified by the sender. More than one person can be specified as a receiver. At least one person must be specified in the **To** field. The initial contents of the **To** field are given by the user in the command (from the shell or **mail's** command mode) to enter the compose mode.

The **Date** field is used to display the date and time that the message was received. The **mail** utility automatically sets the date field.

The **Subject** field is used to describe the message. The **Subject** field is optional and must be provided by the sender.

The **Carbon Copies** field is used to specify who receives a copy of the message. The **Cc** field is optional and must be specified by the sender.

The **Blind Carbon Copies** field is also used to specify who receives a copy of the message. However, the **Bcc** field is not displayed in the message header. People receiving the message do not know who has received a blind carbon copy. The **Bcc** field is optional and must be provided by the sender.

The **Return Receipt To** field is used to specify users who will receive an automatic acknowledgement of the message. The return receipt message simply tells who successfully received the message. The action caused by the **Return Receipt To** field is analogous to sending a registered leter. A record showing that the letter was delivered is obtained; however, no reply message from the recipient is automatically returned.

Note that only those fields that are needed must be specified. The only field that is required by the **mail** utility is the **To** field. The other fields may be used at the sender's discretion.

THE BODY

The body of the message conveys the text of the message. The body can be created using the **mail** utility's compose mode. Alternatively, the body can be made up of an existing file. Such a file could be created using one of the text editors. Generally, short, unformatted messages are created using the compose mode. Messages that are longer or require formatting are usually created with a text editor.

Composing a Message

In this section we discuss how to actually compose a message. Our discussion includes the setting of the header fields and inputting the body of the message.

ENTERING THE mail UTILITY

The command to enter the **mail** utility and start composing a message has the following form:

mail *user name   user name ...*

where *user name* represents the login name of the user who is to receive the message.

For example, the following command:

mail   helen   tom

would cause the **mail** utility to be entered. The compose mode would be active. The users helen and tom would be specified as recipients of the message.

Alternatively, the **mail** utility can be entered by issuing the following command:

mail

If there are no messages in the user's system mailbox, the screen will display:

No Messages

The **mail** utility will then exit and return the user to the shell. If there are messages being held for the user, **mail** will report the number of messages and display information about each one. The command prompt (the underline character) will be displayed. The **m** command may then be used to start composing a message.

The **m** command has the following form:

m *user names*

where *user names* represents list of one or more users.

For example, the following command:

m   helen   tom

would cause the compose mode to be activated. The users helen and tom would be specified as recipients of the message.

SETTING THE TO FIELD

All of the header fields discussed on pages 201 and 202 are set using compose mode escape commands. Compose mode escape commands start with a tilde (~) and are terminated by pressing the Return key. The ~t command is used to add recipients to the **To** field. The ~t command has the following form:

~t *user name   user name ...*

where *user name* represents the login name of a person who is to receive the message.

For example, typing the following:

~t kim

and pressing the Return key would cause the user kim to be added to the list of recipients.

SETTING THE SUBJECT FIELD

The ~s command is used to set the **Subject** field. The ~s command has the following form:

~**s** *text*

where *text* represents the contents of the **Subject** field. The ~s command causes the previous contents of the **Subject** field to be overwritten.

For example, typing the following:

~**s** New summer hours.

and pressing the Return key would cause the subject field to be changed to read "New summer hours."

SETTING THE Cc FIELD

The ~c command adds users to the **Cc** field. The ~c command has the following form:

~**c** *user name   user name ...*

where *user name* represents the login name of each system user who is to receive a copy of the message.

For example, typing the following:

~**c** john laura

and pressing the Return key would cause the users john and laura to be added to the **Cc** field.

SETTING THE Bcc FIELD

The ~b command adds users to the **Bcc** field. The ~b command has the following form:

~**b** *user name   user name ...*

where *user name* represents the login name of each system user who is to receive a blind carbon copy of the message. For example, typing the following:

~b pat scottie

and pressing the Return key would cause the users pat and scottie to be added to the **Bcc** field.

SETTING THE RETURN RECEIPT TO FIELD

The ~**R** command adds users to the **Return Receipt To** field. The ~**R** command has the following form:

~**R** *user name   user name ...*

where *user name* represents the login name of a person who is to receive the return receipt message. Note users should generally only specify themselves as recipients of the return receipt message.

For example, typing the following:

~**R** sully

and pressing the Return key would cause the user sully to be added to the **Return Receipt To** field.

EDITING ALL OF THE HEADER FIELDS

The ~**h** command is used to set or change all of the header fields. The ~**h** command has the following form:

~**h**

This command causes the current setting of each of the header fields to be displayed, one at a time. The current contents of the displayed field can be added to or changed. Pressing the Return key will cause the next field to be displayed.

For example, if the example commands from the preceding sections to set each individual field had been issued, each field would contain the following:

```
To: helen tom kim
Subject: New summer hours.
Cc: john laura
Bcc: pat scottie
Return-receipt-to:sully
```

Typing the following:

~h

and pressing the Return key would cause the following line to be displayed on the screen:

```
To: helen tom kim
```

To add more users to the list, simply type their login names at the tail of the list. To remove someone from the list, simply backspace to the proper name and retype the list. When the Return key is pressed, the screen will display the following:

```
Subject: New summer hours.
```

Once again, the contents of the field can be added to or changed. When the Return key is pressed again, the screen will display:

```
Cc: john laura
```

The **Cc** field can be added to or changed. When the Return key is pressed, the screen will display:

```
Bcc: pat scottie
```

The **Bcc** field can be added to or changed. When the Return key is depressed, the following will be displayed on the screen:

Return-recipt-to:scully

The last time the Return key is depressed, the screen will display:

(continue)

The editing of the header fields is complete. The compose mode is still active.

CREATING THE BODY OF THE MESSAGE

The body of the message is created by simply typing the message. The Return key is used to access a new line. The control-d combination is used to signal the end of the message. When control-d is pressed, the screen will display the following:

(end of message)

The message is then sent to the specified users and the **mail** utility returns to command mode, or exits and returns to the shell, according to how the compose mode was invoked.

USING A PREVIOUSLY CREATED FILE

The body of the message can be taken from a previously created file. Such a file will generally have been created using one of the UNIX text editors.

The ~r command is used to read the file into the body of the message. The ~r command has the following form:

~r *filename*

where *filename* represents the name of the file to be placed into the body of the message.

For example, the following command:

~r memo

would cause the contents of the file **memo** to be placed in the body of the message.

Using the ~r command allows a complicated message that was created using the **ed** or **vi** utilities to be sent via the **mail** utility. Any of the necessary header files can be specified before the message is sent.

MANIPULATING RECEIVED MAIL

Mail received by the individual user should be read and disposed of. Important messages can be saved. Other messages should be deleted. Allowing the mail to stack up is a poor practice because it becomes difficult to find the important messages among the clutter and results in wasted space in the file system.

Received mail is stored in the user's system mailbox. Any user can read the messages while they are in the system mailbox. A personal mailbox, **mbox**, is available. However, the user must transfer the mail from the system mailbox to **mbox** manually.

Entering the mail Utility

When it is time to read the mail, the **mail** utility is invoked by simply typing **mail** and pressing the Return key.

If there are no messages in the user's mailbox, the screen will display:

No Messages.

The **mail** utility will then exit and return the user to the shell. If there are any messages being held for the user, the screen will display a header line followed by a line indicating how many messages are currently in the user's system mailbox. Subsequent lines display the message headers which provide information about each message. Each line is similar to the following line:

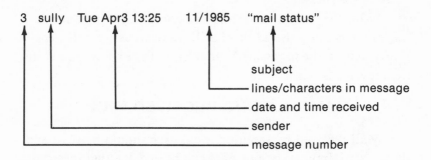

The command mode will be active, indicated by the command prompt, the underline character.

Viewing the Messages

Either the message header, a portion of the message, or the entire message can be displayed. The **h** and **t** commands are useful for finding a particular message. The **p** command is useful for reading an entire message.

MESSAGE NUMBERS

Each message is assigned a number. Generally, the most recently received messages have the highest number. The commands that manipulate the messages, such as viewing, deleting, saving, and responding to mail, all require message numbers as arguments. These message numbers can be referenced in several different manners.

Generally, if no message number is specified, the message that was last acted upon will be affected. We call this default message number the current message. Message numbers can be specified with an actual number or range of numbers. Finally, message numbers can also be specified using the + and - parameters. A + number command will cause the current message number to be changed so that it is closer to the bottom of the list. A - number command will cause the current message number to be changed so that it is closer to the top of the list. Since the messages are listed with the most recent at the top, a - number command will increase the current message number. The first message number is always number one. The last number is represented by a dollar sign. The = command causes the number of the current message to be displayed.

VIEWING THE MESSAGE HEADERS

The **h** command is used to view only the headers of the received messages. The **h** command has the following form:

h *number or range*

where *number* or *range* represents a message number or range of message numbers. The headers of the specified messages will be printed.

For example, the following command:

h 2

would cause the header for the second message to be displayed. Typing only an **h** and pressing the Return key causes all of the headers to be displayed.

DISPLAYING THE FIRST FIVE LINES

The **t** command can be used to view the first five lines of a file. The **t** command has the following form:

t *number or range*

where *number* or *range* represents the message number or range of message numbers of the mail to be displayed.

For example, the following command:

t 5-$

would cause the first five lines of message numbers five through the last message to be displayed.

DISPLAYING THE ENTIRE MESSAGE

The entire message can be displayed using the **p** command. The **p** command has the following form:

p *number*

where *number* represents the message number of the file to be displayed.

For example, the following command:

p +3

would cause the message three places further down the list from the current message to be displayed. If the current message number was five, and no messages had been deleted, then message number 2 would be displayed.

Discarding Unwanted Messages

Messages that have been read and are no longer needed should be deleted from the system. Deleting unneeded messages makes the tasks of handling the remaining mail easier and helps maintain free space within the UNIX file system.

DELETING

The **d** command is used to delete an unneeded message. The **d** command has the following form:

d *number or range*

where *number* or *range* represents a message number or range of message numbers to be deleted. Note that the messages are not renumbered after a delete command. Therefore missing message numbers will reside in the list after several delete commands. The messages will be renumbered the next time the **mail** utility is entered.

For example, the following command:

d +2--1

would cause the following four messages to be deleted:

- The current message
- The two messages before the current message
- The message after the current message.

Note that we used a range of messages instead of specific message numbers. The +2 specifies that two messages before the current message are to be acted upon by the command. The -1 includes the message after the current message in the action. The first dash (-) is the delimiter in the range parameter. Even though the repetition of the dash in the range parameter may appear strange, it is a perfectly valid expression.

UNDELETING

Messages are not actually removed from the file until the **mail** utility is quit. A file deleted earlier in the present **mail** session can still be accessed. The **u** command is used to undelete a file. An undeleted file will once again appear in the message list. The **u** command has the following form:

u *number or range*

where *number* or *range* represents a message number or a range of message numbers.

For example, the following command:

u 7

would cause message number seven to be undeleted. Note that only those messages that are deleted when a quit from **mail** is executed are removed. Messages that are removed are irretrievable.

Saving Messages

Important messages or messages that are awaiting a reply should be saved. There are several places that can be used to store messages. The two standard sites are the system mailbox and the user's personal mailbox. Alternatively, the message can be saved in any UNIX file.

IN THE SYSTEM MAILBOX

The system mailbox is the site where all new messages are delivered. Mail is picked up at the system mailbox when the **mail** utility is invoked without specifying one or more users to send mail to. Each user has a system mailbox. Any messages in the system mailbox can be read by other users, unless the file access permissions are changed (*see* chapter 3, the UNIX File System). The system mailbox should be used to store new messages and messages that are pending some action, such as a reply.

All messages that are not specifically deleted or moved to another location are left in the system mailbox, when a quit is executed.

IN THE USER'S PERSONAL MAILBOX

The user's personal mailbox is a file in the user's home directory. This file is named **mbox**. Messages stored in the **mbox** are no longer accessible to all other users. The **mbox** should be used to store messages that require long term action or messages that must be saved for future reference.

The **mb** command is used to move messages from the system mailbox to the user's **mbox**. The **mb** command has the following form:

mb *number or range*

where *number* or *range* represents a message number or range of message numbers that are to be moved. Note that the actual move will not take place until the **mail** utility is quit.

For example, the following command:

mb 3-4

would cause message numbers three and four to be placed in the **mbox** file.

IN A SPECIFIC FILE

Some messages may need to be stored in a specific UNIX file. For example, a message pertaining to a current project should be stored with that project's files. The **s** or **w** commands are used to move messages to a specific file. The two commands are similar in the actions they perform. We will use the **s** command. However, a **w** command could be substituted for any of the **s** commands. Note that the **w** command causes only the body of the message to be saved. The **s** command has the following form:

s *number or range   filename*

where *number* or *range* represents the message number or range of message numbers that are to be moved and *filename* represents the name of the file to which the message should be appended. Note that if the specified file does not exist, it will be created. If the specified file does exist, the message will be appended at the beginning of the file.

For example, suppose that we have a subdirectory named **proj1** and a file in that directory named **messages**. The following command:

s 1 proj1/messages

would cause message number one to be appended to the **messages** file in the **proj1** subdirectory.

READING SAVED MESSAGES

The **mail** utility may be used to read messages that have been saved in files and to make available all of the **mail** commands for printing headers, deleting, saving etc. The command to do this has the form:

mail -f *filename*

where *filename* is the name of the file containing saved mail messages.

For example, the command:

mail -f mbox

would cause **mail** to access the contents of the file **mbox**.

Responding to Received Mail

Some messages received over the **mail** system require a response. The response may be a reply to the sender or a forwarding of the message to another user. Responding to mail does not cause the message to be deleted from the user's system mailbox.

REPLYING TO THE AUTHOR

The author of a message can be answered using the **r** command. The **subject** field of the message being replied to is placed in the **subject** field of the reply. The compose mode is then activated. The body of the reply is then input in the same fashion as explained in the section on sending mail. The **r** command has the following form:

r *number*

where *number* represents the message number to be replied to. For example, the following command:

r 3

would cause the **To** field to be set to the author of message three. The **subject** field would be set to the **subject** field of message three. The reply can now be composed just as it was when sending original mail. Note that the compose mode escape commands may all be used.

REPLYING TO THE AUTHOR AND ALL RECIPIENTS

The author and all recipients of a message can be replied to using the **R** command. The **R** command causes the header fields of the reply to be copied from the header fields of the message being responded to. Otherwise, the **R** command functions like the **r** command. Note that the people listed in the **Bcc** field of the original message do not get copies of the reply.

FORWARDING A MESSAGE

A message can be forwarded to other users. The body of a forwarded message will contain the header fields and the body of the original message. The actual header fields will specify who forwarded the message and who received copies. The **f** command causes the original message to be indented in the forwarded message. The **F** command allows for no indent. Otherwise, both commands function in the same manner. We shall use the **f** command in our examples. The **F** command could replace any of the **f** commands. The **f** command has the following format:

f number   user names

where *number* represents the number of the message to be forwarded and *user names* represents a list of login names of the users who are to receive copies of the forwarded message.
For example, the following command:

f 2 beth harry

would cause message two to be forwarded to the users beth and harry.

Leaving the mail Utility

The **mail** utility can be left by two methods. Quitting the **mail** utility causes the mail session to be terminated. All changes, such as deletes and moves, are made to the file system. The **q** command is used to quit the **mail** utility. The **q** command has the following form:

q

Exiting the **mail** utility causes the mail session to be terminated. None of the changes are made to the file system. The **x** command is used to exit the **mail** utility. The **x** command has the following form:

x

Generally, the **q** command is used to leave the **mail** utility. The **x** command is generally used when a major error was committed and the current **mail** session must be abandoned.

MISCELLANEOUS FEATURES

In this section we will discuss several additional capabilities of the **mail** utility that did not logically fit into the previous discussions.

Reminders Via mail

The **mail** utility allows the user to set up a reminder service. On the specified dates, a message will be sent to remind the user of an important date or event. The UNIX operating system scans the file named **calendar** in each user's home directory. Lines containing either the current or following day's date are sent via the mail service.

To use the reminder service, a user should create a file named **calendar**. The contents of the file might resemble the following:

> 9/7   First deadline Friday.
> 9/25 Mom's birthday.
> 1/18 Final deadline.

Note that the reminder service requires the **calendar** utility to be run once each day. Consult the system manager to see if this utility is presently included as part of the daily routine.

Hardcopy of a Message

The **l** command is used to obtain a printed copy of a message. The **l** command has the following form:

> **l** *number or range*

where *number* or *range* represents a message number or range of message numbers that are to be printed. The printing is accomplished through the system's **lpr** utility.

Mailing List

A mailing list can be created using the **a** command. The mailing list is referred to as an alias. An alias can be used to refer to several people who are to receive a message, with one name.

Current aliases can be displayed by typing **a** and pressing the Return key. The command to create a new alias has the following form:

> **a** *alias name   user names*

where *alias name* represents the name of the alias to be created and *user names* represents a list of user login names who are to be included in the alias.

For example, the following command:

a proj.1persnl joe linda dennis anne

would cause the alias **proj1.persnl** to be created with members joe, linda, dennis, and anne. Now placing **proj1.persnl** in the **To** field of a message will cause all four of the listed people to receive the message. Aliases set within **mail** are not "remembered" from one mail session to the other. A solution is offered in the "Options" section which will follow.

Using a Text Editor from mail

Both of the editors **ed** and **vi** are available from either the **mail** command or compose mode. From the command mode, the commands to invoke the editors are the following: **v** for **vi** and **e** for **ed**. From the compose mode the commands to invoke the editors are the: ~**v** for **vi** and ~**e** for **ed**.

The dead.letter File

If a message cannot be delivered, it is placed in the **dead.letter** file in the home directory of the sender. Generally, undeliverable messages are caused by an incorrect specification of the receiver. The contents of the message can be salvaged from the **dead.letters** file using the compose mode escape command ~**d**. The command has the following form:

~**d**

This command causes the contents of the **dead.letter** file to be read into the body of the message currently being composed.

Options

As with the **vi** and **ed** utilities many options are available that slightly modify the manner in which the **mail** utility functions. We feel that the **mail** utility functions well without modifying its operation and that a detailed discussion of these options is beyond the scope of an introduction to the **mail** system.

One point about setting options deserves mention. The options are set by commands to **mail**, but rather than setting them by hand each time **mail** is entered, they can be set by a file that is read each time **mail** is invoked. The file, **.mailrc**, is located in the user's home directory. The command syntax is the same as that of commands in command mode. Thus, if the alias command given above were placed in the file **username/. mailrc**, then **proj.persnl** would be available as an alias in every mail session, in both command and compose modes. Other options can automatically prompt for **Subject** and **Cc** fields, or automatically move messages to the **mbox** file. Refer to the system documentation for more information on the available options.

SUMMARY

The following tables provide a command summary for the mail system. We have included commands that we did not discuss for the sake of completeness. Refer to the system documentation for more information about these commands.

Command Mode

Table 7.1. Viewing messages

Command Function	Command Form	Page
View entire next (lower) message.	Press Return key.	—
View nth next (lower) message.	+*number*	211
View nth earlier (higher) message.	—*number*	211
View entire specified message.	**p** *number*	212
View first five lines of specified message.	**t** *number*	212
View headers of message only.	**h** *number*	211

Table 7.2. Manipulating and answering messages

Command Function	Command Form	Page
Delete a message.	**d** *number*	213
Undelete a message.	**u** *number*	214
Edit a message (**ed**).	**e** *number*	221
Edit a message (**vi**).	**v** *number*	221
Forward a message to users (indent).	**f** *number* *user names*	218
Forward a message to users (no indent).	**F** *number* *user names*	218
Hold in mailbox. Used with **autombox** option.	**ho** *number*	—
Print a copy of a message on the system printer.	**l** *number*	220
Move a message to the private mailbox (**mbox**).	**mb** *number*	215

continued on following page

Table 7.2. (cont.) Manipulating and answering messages

Command Function	Command Form	Page
Reply to author of a message. Enter compose mode.	r number	217
Reply to author and all recipients of a message.	R number	218
Append a message to a file.	s number filename	216

Table 7.3. Other command mode commands

Command Function	Command Form	Page
Print number of current message.	=	211
Run a XENIX shell command.	! command	—
Print global aliases.	A	—
Print individual user's aliases.	a	220
Set individual user's aliases.	a alias name user names	220
Change directories.	c directory name	—
Display command list.	list	—
Display command menu help screen.	?	200
Send mail to users. Enter compose mode.	m user names	203
Quit **mail** utility.	q	219
Exit **mail** utility.	x	219
Run a XENIX subshell.	sh	—
Read commands from a file.	so filename	—

continued on following page

Table 7.3. (cont.) Other command mode commands

Command Function	Command Form	Page
Search for a string.	**st** *search string range*	—
Display options help screen.	**set?**	—
Set options.	**set** *options*	—
Unset options.	**unset** *options*	—

Compose Mode

Table 7.4. Specifying message header fields

Command Function	Command Form	Page
Set **subject** field.	~**s** *text*	205
Add users to **To** list.	~**t** *user names*	204
Add users to **Cc** list.	~**c** *user names*	205
Add users to **Bcc** list.	~**b** *user names*	206
Add users to **Return Receipt To** list.	~**R** *user names*	206
Review and edit all header files.	~**h**	206

Table 7.5. Reading in and editing body of message.

Command Function	Command Form	Page
Read in a file.	~**r** *filename*	208
Read in the **dead.letter** file.	~**d**	221
Read in a message (indented).	~**m** *number*	—
Read in a message (not indented).	~**M** *number*	—
Invoke an editor (**ed**).	~**e**	221
Invoke an editor (**vi**).	~**v**	221
Pipe message through a XENIX command.	~**l** *command*	—

Table 7.6. Other compose mode escape commands

Command Function	Command Form	Page
Execute XENIX shell command.	~! *command*	—
Execute **mail** command mode command.	~: *mail command*	—
Begin a line with a tilde.	~~	—
Print global aliases.	~**A**	—
Print individual user's aliases.	~**a**	220
Set individual user's aliases.	~**a** *alias name* *user names*	220
Print contents of message so far.	~**p**	—
Abort message.	~**q**	219
Write message to a file.	~**w** *filename*	—
Display compose mode escape command help screen.	~**?**	200

8

Other Topics

By reading the previous chapters you have gained a working knowledge of the UNIX system. In this chapter, we will introduce a number of other UNIX topics such as job control, printer and terminal control, communications and networking, formatted output and programming languages.

Job Control

UNIX includes a number of commands that allow you to control the programs (or jobs) being executed. In the following sections, we'll discuss three of UNIX's job control commands: & (background), **nohup**, **kill**, and **sleep**.

& (BACKGROUND)

As discussed in chapter 6, when a program is executed in background, the shell remains active. In effect, you can use your terminal while a process is executing independently. & is particularly useful when executing commands which require a long execution time, such as a **sort** with large files.

As shown in the following example, adding & to the end of a command line causes that command to run in background:

```
$sort list a > list b &
5794
$
```

Notice that the background process's PID number is displayed on the screen.

When a process is being run in background, it is a good practice to redirect the output to another file as we did in our example. Otherwise when it finished executing, the background process might direct its output to the screen, which could interrupt your current activities.

A possible problem arises when a long process is executing in background and you want to log out. Logging out could stop the background process's execution. As you'll see in the next section, the **nohup** command allows for completion of the background process even if you log out.

nohup

UNIX's **nohup** command causes jobs started with this command to complete exectuion, even if the user logs out. **nohup** is especially useful if you are using a remote terminal to communicate with the UNIX system using phone lines. The following example illustrates **nohup**:

$nohup sort list a > list b &

If the redirection operator (>) and an output file are not specified, **nohup** will display the following message:

output sent to **nohup.out**

The program's output will be sorted in **nohup.out**.

kill

You can generally stop execution of a program running in foreground by pressing [Control-C]. To stop a program running in background you'll need to execute the **kill** utility. As shown in the following example, executing **kill** with the PID number of the desired process will stop that process's execution.

```
$kill 5794
$
```

If **kill** fails to stop the process's execution, specify **kill** with the **-9** option. **kill -9** is known as the "sure kill."

sleep

UNIX's **sleep** command causes a process to become inactive for a certain period of time. **sleep** is used with the following configuration:

sleep *seconds*

seconds indicates the length of time in seconds that the process will be active. The maximum value for *seconds* is 65,536. An example of **sleep** appears below:

```
$sleep 3600; echo 'Check your mail.' &
```

Here **echo** is executed every hour so that the 'Check your mail.' message is displayed on the terminal.

Communications Among UNIX Systems

All communications discussed thus far have been between users of the same system. Communications with other UNIX systems is also possible.

NETWORKS

Groups of several UNIX systems are referred to as networks. Networks are most commonly attached via phone lines, so the machines do not need to be in close physical proximity to participate in a network.

A network will include facilities for sending mail to a user on a different machine and transferring files to other machines.

Networks range in accessibility from private networks, such as interoffice business networks that are not available to the general public, to national, nonrestrictive networks, such as The Source.

UNIX TO UNIX UTILITIES

Communications between UNIX systems that are not part of a network is accomplished using a special set of utilities. For security reasons, access via these utilities to the remote machine is usually severely limited. A friendly user on the remote machine is quite helpful when trying to accomplish specific tasks on that machine.

The **cu** utility is used to contact another UNIX system. The connection is generally made over the telephone lines using a modem. Before the **cu** utility can be used, information about the remote machine must be known. This information includes the telephone number of the remote system as well as the baud rate and type of parity that will be used for the communication.

Commands starting with **uu** are used to accomplish communication tasks. The following commands are the most useful:

- **uucp**   UNIX to UNIX copy. Can be used to send files to the remote machine or retrieve files from the remote machine.

- **uux**   UNIX to UNIX execute. Allows commands to be executed on a remote machine.

In theory, these commands sound quite useful. In practice, most systems will put severe limitations on the commands and files an outside user can access. This action is taken, and rightly so, for security reasons. Many systems only allow outside users to access the **mail** utility and to send files to the public directory, generally named **uucppublic**.

Text Formatting

In this section we will briefly introduce the subject of text formatting. Primarily, we will discuss the use of the **nroff** utility. The **nroff** utility formats text for output devices such as printers.

Text formatting is the process of changing the appearance of the text. The content of the text is not changed when the text is formatted. Formatting is undertaken to increase the eye appeal of the text. A correctly formatted text gives the final copy a more professional appearance.

INPUT TO nroff

Input to the **nroff** utility is generally one or more files. These files contain the text of the document to be formatted. Embedded within the document are formatting requests. These formatting requests are treated as commands by **nroff**. There are well over 60 such formatting commands. We discuss a few of the formatting requests later in this chapter.

OUTPUT FROM nroff

Output from **nroff** is formatted text. The output from **nroff** is sent directly to the display screen unless a different destination is defined.

INVOKING nroff

The **nroff** utility should be invoked only after the necessary formatting requests have been inserted into the file. The command to invoke **nroff** has the following form:

nroff *-options   filenames*

where *options* represents any of the options listed below and *filenames* represents one or more files that are to be formatted. Note that options are not required. The dash (-) should be excluded if no options are specified. The following options are the more useful of these available:

o*list*   Only selected pages are output.

s   Stops before every page. Used to allow paper loading. Output resumes when the Return key is pressed.

The output from **nroff** can be redirected to another file using the > symbol. The output can be piped to the printer using the following command:

nroff *filename* | **lpr**

SELECTED FORMATTING REQUESTS

In the following sections, we will discuss the more useful formatting requests. Many of the formatting requests that we do not touch upon relate to type font and size. These parameters are used by the **troff** utility, which generates output formatted for a phototypesetter. Such formatting requests do not work well with **nroff** or are simply ignored.

The general form of a formatting request is a period, followed by two characters. A number can usually be specified to change the scope of the command. Generally, if no number is specified, a one (1) is used. Note that all formatting requests are placed on a line that contains only the formatting request. The period must be in the first column. A period in the first column identifies the line as a formatting request to **nroff**.

Before discussing the formatting requests, it is important to note that the **nroff** utility will format text with no imbedded formatting requests. The formatting is executed so that the text fills a standard 8½ x 11 inch sheet. The following is a list of the formatting features that are performed automatically:

- 66 lines per page
- 65 characters per line
- straight left margin
- straight right margin
- single-spaced

PAGE LENGTH

The length of a page of the document can be specified. The page length is always specified as a number of lines. The page length command has the following form:

-pl *number*

where *number* represents the number of lines on the page. If *number* is not present, the page length is set to 66 lines. The page length is usually set at the beginning of the file and only changed for special effects.

For example, the following command:

-pl 54

would cause the page length to be set to 54 lines.

LINE LENGTH

The length of a document line can be set. The line length is always specified as a number of characters. The line length is used to set the left and right margins. The line length command has the following form:

.ll *number*

where *number* represents the number of characters in each line. If *number* is not specified, the line length will be set to 65 characters per line. The line length is usually set at the beginning of the file and changed only for special effects.

For example, the following command:

.ll 50

would cause the line length to be set to 50 characters per line.

LINE SPACING

The .ls command is used to specify the line spacing of the text. The .ls command has the following form:

.ls *number*

where *number* represents the line spacing to be used. If *number* is not specified, the output will be single-spaced.

For example, the following command:

.ls 3

would cause the output to be triple-spaced. The line spacing is usually set at the beginning of the file and changed only for special effects.

FILLING

The **nroff** utility treats a text file as a very long string. It cuts this long string up to form lines. Spaces are added to lines so that the left and right margins are straight. This process is called filling. Note that the **nroff** utility removes the line breaks from the original file and inserts new ones. If the text must appear as it was in the original file, the fill function can be turned off with the **.nf** command. The **.fi** command causes the filling to be resumed. Defeating the fill function is useful when outputting tables.

CENTERING

Certain lines can be centered exactly as they appear in the original file. The **.ce** command is used to center text. The **.ce** command has the following form:

.ce *number*

where *number* represents how many lines should be centered. If *number* is not specified, only one line will be centered.

For example, the following command:

.ce 2

would cause the next two lines to be centered.

PARAGRAPHS

Paragraphs require special handling because they include several irregular features. The last line of a paragraph must not be filled and must be flush left. The first line of the next paragraph must be indented. Sometimes, extra white space must be added between the paragraphs.

The following commands can accomplish these tasks. The **.br** command is used to cause an unconditional break. This causes the line before the break to be filled and flush left.

The **.sp** command is used to insert extra white space into the output. The **.sp** command also causes a break. The **.sp** command has the following form:

.**sp** *number*

where *number* represents the number of blank lines to be inserted into the output.

The **.ti** command causes the next line to be indented. The **.ti** command has the following form:

.**ti** *number*

where *number* represents the number of spaces that the line should be indented.

To specify a paragraph with no extra spacing inserted, the following commands could be used:

```
.br
.ti 5
```

However, most text has many paragraphs. It would be much more convenient if we could specify a paragraph with a single command. We can define our own formatting request with the **.de** command. The **.de** command has the following form:

> **.de** *name*
> *list of formatting commands*

where *name* represents a two-letter name. Note that the name must be different from those already is use.

For example, the following command:

```
.de pa
.br
.fi 5
..
```

would cause the **.pa** command to be defined to accomplish paragraph breaks. The **.pa** command is usually set at the beginning of the file.

Besides saving keystrokes when entering the formatting commands, the definition of a **.pa** command to accomplish paragraph breaks allows the text to be restyled very quickly. For example, the text could be reformed into block style paragraphs by redefining the **.pa** command in the following fashion:

```
.de pa
.sp 2
..
```

EXAMPLE

We now present an example using the simple formatting commands previously discussed. A copy of the original (often called "raw") file follows:

```
.pl 54
.ll 40
.ls 2
.de pa
.br
.ti 5
..
.ce 2
Selected nroff Formatting Requests
Simple Example
.pa
In this example we will show how the
commands that we discussed work.  We
will use all of the commands that we
covered.
.pa
Note that once you get used to using
the text formatter, you can place the
editing commands right in the file as
you go along.  When you are familiar with
this basic set of commands or need
more complex
formatting, consult the system
documentation.
There are many different
commands available.  You
can
accomplish almost any
formatting task using
the XENIX text formatters.
Other formatters include ones for
equations and tables.
.pa
We will now present a short
summary table of the
formatting commands covered
in this discussion.
.sp 4
.ls
.nf
```

Table 12.1. Formatting requests.

Function	Command
Set page length.	.pl #
Set line length.	.ll #
Set line spacing.	.ls #
Turn off fill function.	.nf
Turn on fill function.	.fi
Center lines.	.ce #
Break a line.	.br
Insert white space.	.sp #
Indent the next line.	.ti #
Define a new formatting request.	.de name commands ..

```
.fi
.sp 2
.ls 2
.pa
This is the end of our simple example.
Compare the raw file and the
formatted output.  Note the effect
of the various commands.
```

A copy of the output from **nroff**, printed by a dot matrix printer, follows:

```
       Selected nroff Formatting Requests

             Simple Example

    In this example we  will   show  how

the commands that we discussed work.  We

will use all of  the   commands   that  we

covered.

       Note that  once  you  get  used  to

using  the text formatter, you can place

the editing commands right in  the  file

as  you go along.  When you are familiar

with this basic set of commands or  need

more  complex  formatting,  consult  the

system  documentation.  There  are  many

different  commands  available.  You can

accomplish almost  any  formatting  task

using  the  XENIX text formatters. Other

formatters include  ones  for  equations

and tables.

       We will now present a short summary

table of the formatting commands covered

in this discussion.
```

Table 12.1. Formatting requests.

Function	Command
Set page length.	.pl #
Set line length.	.ll #
Set line spacing.	.ls #
Turn off fill function.	.nf
Turn on fill function.	.fi
Center lines.	.ce #
Break a line.	.br
Insert white space.	.sp #
Indent the next line.	.ti #
Define a new formatting request.	.de name commands ..

This is the end of our simple example. Compare the raw file and the formatted output. Note the effect of the various commands.

Language Utilities

UNIX systems are generally supplied with a number of languages such as C, FORTRAN, Pascal, BASIC, LISP, APL, and Logo. Other languages can generally be added. In the following sections we'll examine the commands used to compile and/or execute programs written in C.

cc — C COMPILER

UNIX's **cc** command is used to compile and load programs written in the C langauge. **cc** is used with the following configuration:

cc [-c -o *filename -l libfile*] *files*

files refers to one or more input files that contain a C source program (with a filename extension of .c) or a C object code file (with a filename extension of .o).

In its most elementary form, **cc** compiles its C source file argument into an executable file named **a.out**. **cc** places the object program in a file with the filename of the specified input file and the extension .o. If only one C program is being compiled, the object program is deleted. For example,

cc pgml.c

would place an executable version of **pgml.c** in **a.out**. You could later run this program by entering **a.out**.

The -c option causes **cc** to compile the C program file and place the object program in a file with the input filename specified and the extension .o. The object file is not loaded.

-o *filename* causes the executable program to be placed in a file named *filename* rather than **a.out**.

-l *libfile* causes the specified library file to be loaded.

An object file can be combined with a program file using **cc**. This is especially useful if you wish to add to or modify a C program which has already been compiled without entirely recompiling it.

For example,

cc -o pgm2   pgmla.c   pgml.o

compiles **pgmla.c** into **pgmla.o** and combines this with **pgml.o**. This object file is then loaded to create an executable file named **pgm2**.

Appendix A

Appendix A.
UNIX Command Summary

Command	Description
awk	Search for a pattern within a file. Includes a built-in programming language.
bdiff	Compares two large files.
bfs	Scans a large file.
cal	Displays a calendar.
cat	Concatenates and prints files.
cc	C compiler.
cd	Change directory.
chgrp	Changes a file's group ownership.
chmod	Changes a file's access permissions.
chown	Changes the individual ownership of a file.
cmp	Compares two files; displays the location (line and byte) of the first difference between these.
comm	Compares two files so as to determine which lines are common to both.
cp	Copies a file to another location.
cu	Calls another UNIX system.
date	Returns the date and time.
df	Displays free space in the file system.
diff	Displays the differences between two files or directories.
diff3	Displays the differences between three files or directories.

continued on following page

Command	Description
du	Reports on file system usage.
echo	Displays its argument.
ed	Text editor.
ex	Text editor.
expr	Evaluates its argument which is generally a mathematical formula.
f77	FORTRAN compiler.
find	Locates the files with specified characteristics.
format	Initializes a floppy disk.
grep	Searches for a pattern within a file.
help	Provides help.
kill	Ends a process.
ln	Used to link files.
lpr	Copies the file to the line printer.
ls	Displays information about one or more files.
mail	Used to receive or deliver electronic messages.
mkdir	Creates a new directory.
more	Displays a long file so that the user can scroll through it.
mv	Used to move or rename files.
nroff	Used to format text.
ps	Display a process's status.
pwd	Display the name of the working directory.
rm	Removes one or more files.

continued on following page

Command	Description
rmdir	Deletes one or more directories.
sleep	Causes a process to become inactive for a specified length of time.
sort	Sort and merge one or more files.
spell	Finds spelling errors in a file.
split	Divides a file.
stty	Display or set terminal parameters.
tail	Displays the end of the file.
troff	Outputs formatted output to a typesetter.
tset	Sets the terminal type.
umask	Allows the user to specify a new creation mask.
uniq	Compares two files. Finds and displays lines in one file that are unique.
uucp	UNIX-to-UNIX execute.
vi	Full screen editor.
wc	Displays details in the file size.
who	Displays information on the system users.
write	Used to send a message to another user.

Index